Seaside

Edited by David Mohney and Keller Easterling

Princeton Architectural Press

Sea

Seaside: Making a Town in America
Edited by David Mohney and Keller Easterling
Princeton Architectural Press

side

Wesley: You don't understand what's happening yet, do you?

Emma: With what?

Wesley: The house. You think it's Mr. and Mrs. America who're gonna' buy this place, but it's not. It's Taylor.

Emma: He's a lawyer.

Wesley: He works for an agency. Land development.

Emma: So what?

Wesley: So it means more than losing the house. It means losing a country.

Emma: You make it sound like an invasion.

Wesley: It is. It's a zombie invasion. Taylor is the head zombie. He's the scout for the other zombies. He's only a sign that more zombies are on their way. They'll be filing through the door pretty soon.

Emma: Once you get it built.

Wesley: There'll be bulldozers crashing through the orchard. There'll be giant steel balls crashing through the walls. There'll be foremen with their sleeves rolled up and blueprints under their arms. There'll be steel girders spanning acres of land. Cement pilings. Prefab walls. Zombie architecture, owned by invisible zombies, built by zombies for the use and convenience of all other zombies. A zombie city! Right here! Right where we're living now.

Sam Shepard, *The Curse of the Starving Class* (1976)

For Glenn and Elaine, and Marcia and Dudley

Book design: Michael Bierut
Production editor: Stefanie Lew

Special thanks to: Sheila Cohen, Scott Corbin,
Antje Fritsch, Clare Jacobson, Kevin C. Lippert,
and Ann C. Urban.

© 1991 Princeton Architectural Press, Inc.
94 93 92   5 4 3 2

Cover photo: Steven Brooke
Photography credits for color introduction: Michael Moran, except
pages 24–25: Steven Brooke

Library of Congress Cataloguing-in-Publication Data
Seaside : making a town in America / edited by David Mohney and
Keller Easterling.
    p.   cm.
ISBN 1-878271-44-x (cloth) : $39.95
ISBN 0-910413-26-6 (paper) : $24.95
1. Architecture—Florida—Seaside—Themes, motives. 2. Seaside
(Fla.)—Buildings, structures, etc. 3. New towns—Florida. 4. City
planning—Florida—Seaside—History—20th century.
I. Mohney, David, 1953–   . II. Easterling, Keller, 1959–   .
NA735.S44S43 1991   91–4302
720'.9759'41—dc20   CIP

Published by
Princeton Architectural Press, Inc.
37 East 7th Street
New York, New York 10003
212.995.9620

Contents

David Mohney

Preface and Acknowledgements

Cities, even if they last for centuries, are in reality great encampments of the living and the dead where a few elements remain like signals, symbols, warnings. When the holiday is over, the elements of the architecture are in tatters, and the sand again devours the street. There is nothing left to do but resume, with persistence, the reconstruction of elements and instruments in expectation of another holiday.
Aldo Rossi, *A Scientific Autobiography* (1981)

In December 1984, I went to Seaside for the first time. There were only a dozen or so buildings to see, mostly houses, along just one street that stretched back from the state highway and away from the beach. Six and one-half years (and five more trips) later, much has changed: not only are there more than one hundred built houses, but also there exist enough commercial buildings to clearly define the town center. It is, however, the evolutionary nature of this substantial growth, rather than the accumulation of new buildings, which has sustained my interest in Seaside, and has produced this book and the exhibition that preceded it.

Even during that first visit, it was unmistakable that Seaside was a serious attempt to address the issue of the public realm in contemporary American society. This sense was dramatically reinforced from the beginning simply by the drive to the town. If one arrives in Seaside driving along the coast, either west from Panama City or east from Pensacola, the sheer magnitude of the change in the American landscape over the last forty years—a result of the automobile—is overwhelming. A plethora of strip malls, repetitive housing units, and jumbled pseudo-styles ignore everything except the highway and their connection to it. Sometimes, as Robert Venturi noted, that can be all right: in the center of the honky-tonk beach resorts like Panama City, there is a pleasantly tacky kind of urbanism that results from the dense concatenation of these single-minded elements (and the imposition of a pedestrian scale). But the problem comes at the edges, or rather, lack of edges, of these places, where the density no longer prevails, and single-mindedness turns to simple-mindedness, stretching on for mind-numbing mile after mile.

In contrast, when approaching Seaside from inland, coming through certain older towns like DeFuniak Springs, Florida, or Eufaula, Alabama, the landscape is vastly different. There is no single-minded focus in these towns, and the buildings have been adapted, over time, to each other. There is a rich diversity of settings for human experience, from the town square to the highway service district to the variety of residential neighborhoods. The buildings and public spaces have been made to reflect and respect each other, and that history of change and accommodation is the most tangible manifestation of the authentic urbanism of those towns.

It is towns like these that have provided the prototypes for Seaside's neighborhoods. Looking around a town like Eufaula, for example, one recognizes the elements of Seaside's genealogy. Andres Duany and Elizabeth Plater-Zyberk's powers of observation are such that they not only found the appropriate prototypes, but understood how to codify the elements of the types in a manner that would allow for creativity in composing new structures. Best of all, they saw and understood, clearly, the value of a sense of place shared (or reinterpreted, and thus reinforced) by many different points of view.

Too often we measure urbanism in terms of our human circumstances, when in fact it should be considered on a scale suitable to its own particular exigencies. These can vary widely. In the 1980s, development that was nearly instantaneous seemed to be a success, but usually these projects were cases of extreme single-mindedness. From that point of view, Seaside is a complete anomaly in that it took nearly a decade to build a hundred different houses. But within

1.
High-rise condominium building between the beach and the highway, near Panama City, Florida
2.
Row-house condominiums near Panama City
(Photos: David Mohney)

Seaside itself, the waves of building activity, which manifested themselves in a succession of stylistic changes every two years or so, pointed to something else: the genesis of a history, no less authentic for its compression, that transcends the simple growth of the town.

Now I understand why Seaside has seemed to be a different place each time I have visited it. On my first trip, at the end of 1984, in addition to just one street paved with crushed oyster shells and a dozen houses, there were a number of public structures: a beach pavilion, a gazebo, and even a small park with garden furniture including a chess pavilion. And thus a balance existed between the individuality of the buildings and the community of the street. The public buildings existed for a real public. Despite the fact that it was only two blocks long and by no means complete, that street was the street of a town, not a development, not an isolated vacation retreat, not a planned community. Bulldozed lines in the sand, indicating the streets to come, only reaffirmed the promise of what had been built.

By my second trip, in mid-1986, there were two streets existing side-by-side. The public realm was still balanced between the private houses and the public streets, with mediation provided by a growing number of public structures. The third trip, in the spring of 1987, was probably the most disappointing for me: three adjacent residential streets were largely built up, but the central square remained undefined. The residential streets themselves had been paved with brick, which gave them a finished quality. This, in effect, gave the impression that Seaside was complete,

3–4.
Houses in DeFuniak Springs, Florida
Vernacular houses in small towns
throughout the South provided the
prototypes for the development of the
Seaside Urban Code
(Photos: Neil Levine)

and could be perceived in one glance. The assemblage of residential buildings seemed to create a contained community, without a civic or commercial center. My fourth trip, late in 1988, changed that perception because the first major building on the square had been started: a downtown was in the making. Two additional streets of houses were underway, and a series of stylistic reactions to a latent Victorian style of the previous street (see the work of Chatham and Casasco with respect to that of Cohen and Nereim, for example) was in full force.

By mid-1989, construction had started on the west side of town, reinforcing the centrality of the town square. And most recently, in 1990, you could turn a corner at Seaside and, for the first time, have the town turn the corner with you. How Seaside will evolve remains a pertinent question, but as the 1990s start, I can say that Seaside is no longer in the process of becoming a town. It *is* a town.

This book owes a large part of its existence to the Institute for Architecture and Urban Studies (now defunct). The idea for the exhibition and catalogue started there, after I invited Andres Duany to give a lecture about Seaside in 1984. I offer thanks to the trustees who supported the IAUS, especially John Burgee and Philip Johnson, whose support for the exhibition was steadfast from its inception through its planning and execution. Edie Morrill administered the IAUS through this period with skill. Others from the IAUS whose help and encouragement I wish to acknowledge are Mario Gandelsonas, Anthony Vidler, Paul Gates, Deborah Gans, Lynne Breslin, and Joel Sanders.

3

4

39

5.
Eufaula, Alabama
Town center
6.
Eufaula, Alabama
Vernacular prototype for Seaside's
central square (Type I): a two-story
arcade faces the main intersection in
the town
(Photos: David Mohney)

5

6

With the Seaside exhibition in the final stages of preparation, the IAUS closed its doors in the summer of 1985. The Architectural League stepped in, sponsored the exhibition (which was held at the Urban Center Gallery in New York), and organized its subsequent tour around the country. For this, many thanks are owed to Frances Halsband, then President, as well as to Elizabeth Feeley and Anne Rieselbach. Rosalie Genevro, the League's Administrative Director, deserves enormous recognition for helping us at a time when it was truly needed, and for doing so in the most graceful and thorough manner.

I have asked many people at Seaside for help over the last five years, and all have responded kindly: Carmel Modica, Nancy Patrie, Zoann Merrill, Scott Merrill, and especially John Seaborn, Pam Watkins, and Beth Fulta. All of the designers, architects, owners, and builders represented in the book provided materials as requested. At Princeton Architectural Press, Clare Jacobson, Ann Urban, and Amy Weisser provided assistance; Stefanie Lew supervised the production with thorough and gracious professionalism; and Kevin Lippert assisted this project with tremendous patience. There are others who helped: Carol Willis shared her valuable insights on the subject and helped mount the exhibition in New York; Mark Magowan provided important professional counsel; Michael Bierut designed the book with everyone looking over his shoulder, and managed to satisfy all (he also designed the graphics and flyer for the exhibition). The essayists, Kurt Andersen and Neil Levine, gave their writing their complete and valued attention. The primary photographers, Steven Brooke and Michael Moran, were generous with their professional sensibilities.

7

7.
Tupelo Street gazebo, Seaside
December 1984
8.
Seaside exhibition at the Urban
Center galleries, New York
August–September 1985
(Photos: David Mohney)

From the Chan and Mohney office, Nate Cherry, Ann Krsul, David Levine, James Mandle, Antonia Salazar, and Joseph Sultana, Jr. assisted with production. Both Keller and I wish to thank Robert Gutman for his encouragement and inspiration.

The planners and developer of Seaside regard the town as an on going experiment. This book documents and reflects its growth. It should be pointed out that the projects shown here represent what Keller Easterling and I believe to be a thorough sampling of what has been built or designed for Seaside, not a complete catalogue. As Seaside continues to evolve, we have every intention of continuing our investigation and evaluation of it, and thus updating this volume as conditions warrant.

My greatest appreciation must go to Robert and Daryl Davis, and Andres Duany and Elizabeth Plater-Zyberk, who had the vision to begin an experiment along a beach in the Florida panhandle and who have had the continuing patience to wait uncompromisingly for the outcome. They have also cheerfully assisted this project throughout its lengthy history. Finally, I offer my sincere appreciation to my co-editor, Keller Easterling, and to my partner, Joan Chan. I hope they all feel this volume has been worth the wait.

8

Kurt Andersen

Is Seaside Too Good To Be True?

1.
Andres Duany and
Elizabeth Plater-Zyberk
(Photo: Pelham Photo)

Is Seaside too good to be true? If the story of its creation were fiction, we would find it facile, cloying, implausibly romantic. *The former sixties-radical son of an Alabama Jewish mercantile family becomes a Florida real-estate developer, and gets the notion to turn his grandfather's scrubby Gulf Coast tract into an architecturally ambitious resort community for enlightened Southerners. He hires a brilliant young husband-and-wife team (he a charismatic son of refugees from communist Cuba, she the cerebral daughter of refugees from communist Poland, their mentor an eccentric London-based classicist who had never built a thing) to design an old-fashioned Southern town from scratch. A scant decade later, total victory: the new town, already more than half finished, is a popular and critical success, influential among architects, planners, and developers. The husband-and-wife team, meanwhile, are barnstorming America, overseeing the creation of a dozen more such towns— and helping to plan another in England for their devoted new client, the Prince of Wales! Finally, the London mentor, having provided both inspiration and occasional comic relief all along, has seen fit to build his first building—a house for himself, right in the middle of Seaside—and flies in to carry his wife across the threshold. Smiles, laughter, warm feelings all around. The end.* Ridiculous. But the tale is entirely true, of course; the basic facts by now familiar. Robert Davis really is a benign despot. Andres Duany and Elizabeth Plater-Zyberk, 40 and 39 years old respectively, really do wield more influence than any other architects of their generation. Leon Krier, the classicist guru, really does have a brand new clapboard house in the middle of the Florida Panhandle. And Seaside—fetching, rigorous, quirky, humane—is, miraculously, a real place.

Thinking about Seaside, it is hard not to be amazed. It's amazing to witness such a thoroughgoing and successful break with years of urban planning orthodoxy and complacency. Conventional suburban developments (amorphous strings of houses too densely built to be rural, too scattered to be urban, with too-wide, pointlessly winding streets that make navigation difficult and walking unthinkable) have looked the way they look for more than a generation. The so-called Planned Unit Development (PUD), where more than one out of ten Americans live, now has the force of law, economics, and popular custom behind it; envisioning any practical alternative had become nearly impossible. Great suburbs may have been built in the past, went the defeatist truism, but they are impossible to build now. Duany and Plater-Zyberk have proven otherwise: they are the first radical critics of modern sprawl who did more than just decry and bemoan; they sufficiently understood the nuts and bolts of how PUD suburbs came to be—the zoning, the infrastructure, the traffic engineering, the cost of money—to mount an effective campaign of subversion.

It's amazing that the premise of Seaside—that America's eighteenth- and nineteenth-century towns remain great models of urban coherence and felicity—is so simple, even obvious, and yet was so willfully neglected for fifty years. It is as if, around 1945, Americans had given up something as fundamental and wholesome as bread, deciding the stuff was too old-fashioned, too complicated and time-consuming to bake—and then, suddenly, several decades later, came to realize that they loved bread and still had the recipe on file. Yet in an era mad for recycling bits of the past, Duany and Plater-Zyberk were among the few revivalists who looked beyond the superficial. True, residents and visitors are fond of Seaside partly (maybe

2

43

largely) for the reproductions of the fifty- and one-hundred-year-old styles, but it is the master planners' subtler urban traditionalism—the town center, the civic buildings, the street grid and narrow streets, the lot sizes, alleys, and setbacks—that distinguishes Seaside from scores of instantly erected ersatz-old-fashioned places.

It's amazing that a scheme so quixotic is working out pretty much as planned. This is due partly to Davis's wisdom and tenacity, but also to Duany and Plater-Zyberk, who, unlike most architectural visionaries (including Krier), are clear-eyed pragmatists who would never be satisfied with mere drawing-board perfection. Duany especially seems a politician by temperament, inspiring, wheedling, arguing, acquiring allies. It's amazing—or at least ironic—that such a sweet, earnest, idealistic project would come to fruition in the bombastic, cynical, anti-utopian 1980s. Not since the anything-is-possible-in-Camelot days of the early sixties—with the new towns of Reston and Columbia rising just beyond the Beltway, and urban renewal in its debased Pruitt-Igoe/Lincoln Center forms not quite discredited—have so many naturally skeptical people been excited by a planning scheme.

Indeed, Seaside was in several senses made possible by the 1960s. As the wrong-headedness of postwar planning started to become clear (as Leon Krier said recently, the modernists failed "to make towns and villages . . . that people want to come from"), Jane Jacobs looked closely at just what makes for successful urban neighborhoods and used her research to argue compellingly in *The Death and Life of Great American Cities* (1961) for a rediscovery of dense, tried-and-true vitality—just as Duany and Plater-Zyberk are doing now with small towns and suburbs. At the same time, Robert Venturi made vernacular forms respectable, and granted serious architects permission to dip into classicism. Duany and Plater-Zyberk, a generation later, have sought to use those freedoms more thoughtfully and ambitiously than most of Venturi's putative heirs. Seaside is a heartening and important postmodernist residue, for Duany and Plater-Zyberk applied the best, deepest lessons of the reaction against modernism—the pleasures of materials, the virtues of familiar forms and small scale. And there is a whiff of the late sixties in Seaside's particular evocation of the good life: Krier's Luddite dreams were provoked by Europe's 1968 student rebellion, and the countercultural pasts of Davis and his archetypal residents now manifest themselves in Seaside's quasi-populist architectural style; in its celebration of community and nature; in its affluent, overeducated, hang-loose, good vibes.

Seaside has provoked opposition, much of it knee-jerk grousing. Avant-gardists and diehard modernists naturally reject the embrace of tradition, although the Seaside architectural code's recent accommodation of tough, idiosyncratic structures (the commercial buildings by Steven Holl and Deborah Berke at the center of town, Walter Chatham's house) tends to disarm those critics. Another complaint is that Seaside is precious, simply too perfect. Is there any way around this in a new town? The planners and developer have gone to great lengths to encourage authentic heterogeneity: they've taken almost ten years to build just the first half of Seaside, an extraordinarily long time for a project of this size; Duany and Plater-Zyberk have heroically refrained from designing a single

3.
Windsor
Town-planning project by Duany and
Plater-Zyberk, near Vero Beach,
Florida, 1989
(Photo: Duany / Plater-Zyberk)

4.
Charleston Place
Subdivision design and buildings by
Duany and Plater-Zyberk, near Boca
Raton, Florida, 1980
(Photo: Duany / Plater-Zyberk)

5.
Wellington
Town-planning project by Duany and
Plater-Zyberk, near West Palm
Beach, Florida, 1989
(Photo: Duany / Plater-Zyberk)

3

4

5

45

building; and, so far, only one architect has designed more than a dozen houses. But the diversity, although genuine, is still the result of a closely administered master plan—a certain self-consciousness, even smugness, is inevitable. (What other village of several hundred inhabitants, after all, has a book devoted to it?) Under these circumstances, normalcy takes time to achieve; fifty years from now, Seaside will have ceased to be a hothouse curiosity, and will become just another charming American town.

Other critics complain that it is elitist, a colony of second homes where a tyranny of good taste reigns. Well, yes; like most new architecture of merit, the patrons are well-to-do, and the site all but required that it be a resort town. But give the place a break: Seaside strives to avoid pernicious elitism. There is no grand gate or guardhouse, no security fence. The required vernacular forms and materials mean that ostentation is almost impossible. The public buildings are small and simple. Of course Seaside is fundamentally an exercise in nostalgia, seeking (like practically every suburb in the country) to indulge middle-class Americans' pastoral urges. The miracle is that (unlike practically any suburb in the country) it manages to conjure the good old days impeccably, solidly, jauntily, even profoundly.

Because Seaside came into existence during the 1980s, and because it is in concept and style conservative— radically conservative—many of its critiques take a leftist political tack. Davis and his planners and architects may not be Reaganites, the argument goes, but they are complicit in today's whole retrograde cultural agenda. This can make for interesting theoretical discussion; however, Seaside is conservative in the best sense: there

is a return to town-planning principles, architectural novelty for its own sake is strongly discouraged (but not quite outlawed), urban discipline and coherence are maintained without a deadening uniformity. Furthermore, the engine of Seaside and its successors—Duany and Plater-Zyberk's succinct codes that regulate the size, placement, materials, and basic shapes of buildings—is not mysterious or arcane, and is thus democratic; regular citizens can understand how and why it works. What are Seaside's politics? The codes reinforce individual privacy (picture windows and sliding glass doors are prohibited) except when it diminishes the sense of community (houses must be close to the street and each other). It is conservative, and it is democratic; it is elitist, and it is populist; it is American.

Duany and Plater-Zyberk have utopian aspirations that are yet to be realized. In their newer new towns—such as The Kentlands in Maryland, which will be four or five times as big as Seaside—they plan to have some real human diversity, mixing ages and socio-economic classes and uses (including one million square feet of office space) to a degree that Seaside doesn't attempt. The pair's influence is extending well beyond the developments they personally plan: the Traditional Neighborhood Development ordinance they've written and for which they continually proselytize is a generic, boilerplate document that local governments can adopt wholesale, replacing the current laws and regulations that result in charmless subdivisions and overburdened highways. (It is the nation's traffic engineers, by the way, who have a large professional stake in the status quo—driving is good, driving fast on big roads is best—

6

7

and who are by far the most powerful opponents that the traditional-neighborhood movement faces. And it has become a movement.)

The 1990s may be ripe for the Seaside model to proliferate, for the old-fashioned, densely built, small-scale, mixed-use, pro-pedestrian approach to become the American planning paradigm. If this new decade lives up to the early line—a return to hearth and home, a commitment to environmentalism, more coherent, more humble, kinder, gentler—then Seaside, a strange one-of-a-kind jewel in the eighties, may turn out to have been a preview of the nineties and beyond. Or so, anyway, it is no longer madness to hope.

Portions of this essay appeared in Time *magazine.*

Keller Easterling

Public Enterprise

There are really three parties to every land subdivision: the owner or operator, the prospective user (owner or tenant), and the public. It would represent a great advance if we could come to look upon these parties as partners with certain interests in common in the proper subdivision of land.[1]
John Nolen, *City Planning* (1924)

Seaside's real value has often been invisible in photography and press coverage. The town's chief innovation has less to do with its buildings and more to do with the space between the buildings and the buildings' response to that space.

Our sense of American urban traditions and the history of suburbia's devolution in the twentieth century is rather amnesic. Typically separated from the process of making a town, we are often bewildered by the seemingly accidental proportions of residential communities. The taxonomy of American urban types requires precise distinctions concerning morphology, politics, and various indeterminate qualities associated with a community's growth over time. Seaside stands at the beginning of a thorough reexamination of town, suburb, and region in America. The town begins by offering an alteration of the residential street and neighborhood that aspires to the most elusive, but potentially the sturdiest, of all of America's urban traditions—the garden-variety small town.

The New "Briarhaven"
The generic post-World War II suburban subdivision is not a town or community but rather a large tract of privately owned land overlaid with curving streets and a platting plan. Typically, the planning of these subdivisions relies on common standards of real-estate development or traffic engineering. Streets are not intended as public thoroughfares, and they are often composed with excessive widths and deadened front yards that are unrelieved by shared landscaping or other street fixtures. Designing the houses that inhabit this landscape has become a formulaic exercise related to expedient and generalized standards of value set by

developers and financial institutions. Rarely, if ever, are a variety of uses or building types integrated into the residential fabric; rarely, if ever, is there a provision for shared open space. One tract is distinguished from another by an assigned name like "Briarhaven." Briarhaven represents the great experiment in affordable living that made its imprint on the American landscape since World War II.

In the 1980s a new Briarhaven has developed, or rather Briarhaven has been given a new name. Today the housing product is made more attractive and exclusive with image. The new "profession" of the marketing consultant helps to insure sales by selecting the correct image to attract the correct "target market." The image may be nostalgic, futuristic, exotic, or "neo-small town," and it is concocted from a variety of accoutrement: luxury recreation facilities, elaborate surveillance security systems, cosmetic architectural styling, or perhaps nothing more than the suggestion of image through name. Though Briarhaven's "new features" are valued only according to the most recent financially successful development, the valuation methods are often treated with the respect of a science. Marketing studies help to perpetuate a set of needs and desires that replaces the American urban tradition with a fiction about home and civic life that can be packaged and sold.

Often the new Briarhaven is composed of a series of cul-de-sacs on a large arterial wrapped around a golf course. The arterial, as the only throughway for the automobile, is thus sized to accommodate peak loads and is rarely rendered as a pedestrian way. The common landscape—the golf course—is largely impenetrable to pedestrians. So while there is the

1

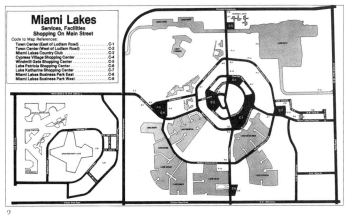

2

Las Colinas, Texas provides a somewhat extravagant example of the new Briarhaven. It is built around a cluster of skyscrapers and served by an artificial canal system. Residents are only a motor boat ride away from the office tower, country club, and mock Mexican shopping village. The "headquarters" of Las Colinas is really a quasi-governmental control station for the electronic surveillance system. Many people who work in Las Colinas, however, cannot afford to live there and take advantage of the home-to-office canal excursion. Those that do might prefer to forego that pleasure in deference to the arterial highway which is the real connector between the

illusion of the public park and the public thoroughfare there are only limited ways for each resident of each cul-de-sac to make his way through the town—usually in a car from cul-de-sac to arterial and back again. This method of development is not derived from the science of community planning, but rather results from ideas about expedient phasing and reduced infrastructure costs. The environment is maintained typically by private condominium or homeowners' associations. The new Briarhaven is composed of the same ingredients as it predecessor with perhaps an increasing emphasis on the exclusion of public land and public life. Still, these subdivisions are advertised with the new title: "Briarhaven: A Planned Community."
The Briarhavens of yesterday and today have been accused of creating isolated and homogeneous communities and of exacerbating environmental abuses. Moreover, private community governments, such as those condominium and homeowners' associations that control the new Briarhavens, outnumber the elected governments of towns, counties, and municipalities in the United States.[2]

A Changing Suburban Morphology

Throughout its history, suburbia has been, at times, the vehicle for progressive ideologies and radical politics, but it has almost always involved the negotiation of property or the consumption of the house and lot as product. Most of our "traditions" have been rendered, at some point, with a degree of artifice and fiction to promote sales. Today's city, suburb, and region would be well informed by a critical and precise examination of the history of these urban traditions and political processes, research that distinguishes the radical

3

4

separate development pods. Barring the chance passing of two water taxis, there is little likelihood that neighbors will meet casually within the town. One is more likely to socialize in private clubs or at home. Most communities like Las Colinas guarantee the resident a similar brand of protected solitude.

5.
Comparative lot sizes
Post-war suburbs aspired to an aesthetic similar to that of early suburbs; however, the overall size of suburban communities typically increased as the lot size decreased.

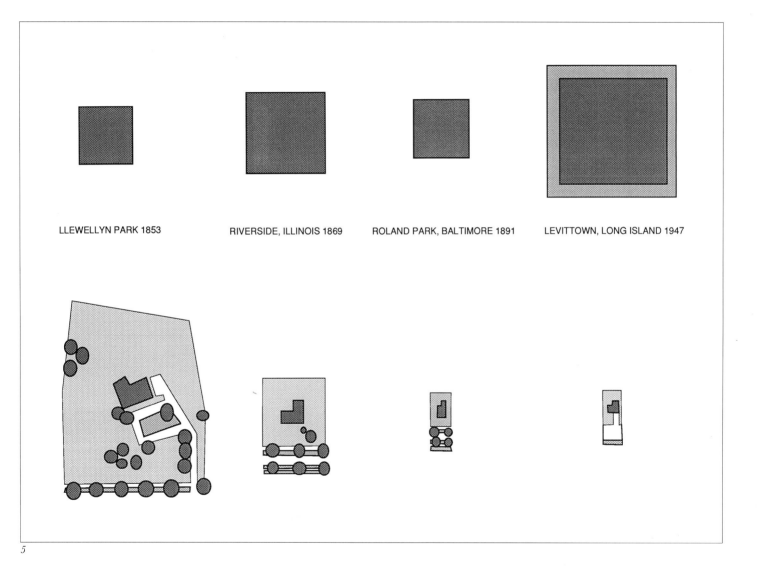

LLEWELLYN PARK 1853   RIVERSIDE, ILLINOIS 1869   ROLAND PARK, BALTIMORE 1891   LEVITTOWN, LONG ISLAND 1947

5

The cul-de-sac, as used in both the old and the new Briarhaven, derives from the regionalist planning science of the twenties and thirties. Extracted piecemeal by the Federal Housing Administration and used in promoting post-war housing, the cul-de-sac lost its specialized functions in the context of the science as a whole and gradually became just another generic street type. This is perhaps consistent with the government's apparent disregard for the great planning experiments of the early twentieth century and for a generation of planners whose science had matured over the period from City Beautiful planning to the emergence of regionalist planning.

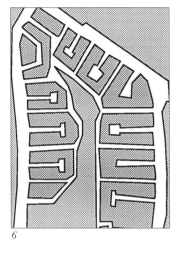

6

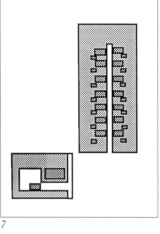

7

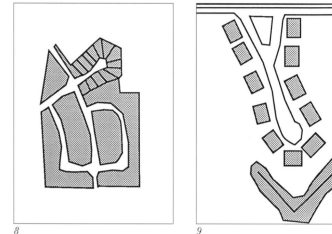

8

9

diagram from the product and the product from the fiction. The diverse catalogue of morphologies in Briarhaven's history defies a unifying utopianism and unmasks the increasingly formulaic seventies and eighties suburb with its advertised claims of "authenticity" as one of the most profoundly amnesic chapters in the history of suburbia.

The issue concerning the ratio of public space to private space in the subdivision of land for residential purposes, on the scale of the street or the region, confronts America's fundamental attitudes regarding property and ecology.

The Small Town

In an aerial view of our urban fringes, amidst the virulent growth of Briarhavens, stand some of the last remaining examples of what we customarily call the American small town. It may be a courthouse town with a central square or it may be a town composed of only a small grid of streets next to a river or a railway line; the American small town is really a changing series of hybrids. There are the New World and colonial settlements, the gridirons of American expansion, examples of City Beautiful planning, and American versions of the Garden City.

The small town is a special form of urbanism, distinct from the big city, with its own forces to regulate size, growth, and the formation of the public domain. It defies a rational formal analysis; understanding its structure requires careful examination of spatial experience as well as plan diagram. A town's evolution depends on holding in solution a number of pivotal events against elements in flux. This may be due in part to erratic patterns of growth. Some towns have developed under controlled conditions; some under more anarchic conditions. Landscape in the small town—for instance, the row of trees lining the residential street—is largely responsible for creating the public domain against which private statements of property are made.[3]

As one of the most fundamental structures of small town urbanism and the first meeting ground of public and private space, the residential street illustrates on a

52

small scale some of the properties of the town as a whole. Michael Dennis writes about the "quintessential tree-lined residential street."[4] He traces the roots of "Elm Street" back to the Jeffersonian model of the neoclassical pavilion in a romantic landscape which "had the potential to serve as the ideal fabric of civilized agrarian democracy."[5] Elm Street and its Jeffersonian roots have achieved mythic proportions in America.

This attitude toward building and landscape, so clearly diagrammed in Jefferson's University of Virginia, is also illustrated by Elm Street as a series of detached houses on a common turf. Dennis writes:

Here public and private are both accommodated in a respectful dialogue; and adherence to the conventions of street, sidewalk, front yard, porch, and public rooms is precisely what allows for the possibility of invention and private variation.

Unfortunately, the very characteristics that give the small American town its positive qualities are also those which make it extremely vulnerable. Endless nuance and interpretation are possible as long as the delicate balance of solids and voids is maintained. But the Neoclassical system is inherently biased in favor of the private icon, so balance is doubly dependent on maintenance of the public realm, the underpinnings of which are still, however faint, those of the classical structure of space—of street and square. What is not defined by the buildings must be completed by the trees, and the slight weakening of either element can result in serious erosion of the system.[6]

The same interdependence that exists between building and landscape and between the public and private realm in the small town must also inform the partnership between developer, designer, and citizen. Throughout our history private concerns have traditionally sold lots rather than street and public spaces. Successful schemes usually respond to the developer's profit motive by increasing the value of the property. Elm Street and other structures of the small town are complex physical manifestations of the ongoing negotiations between the public and private parties to community. Though the latest forms of suburban development threaten to supplant some of our last remaining models, the small town invites reinterpretation and stands with a legacy of solutions awaiting the keen vision and sensitivity to recover them.

Seaside, Florida

It is just such a rediscovery of American small-town urbanism that informs the plan of Seaside, Florida, designed by the firm of Andres Duany and Elizabeth Plater-Zyberk Architects in close cooperation with the owner and developer, Robert Davis. Through a series of favorable accidents they began altering the pieces of a typical residential development and arrived at a scheme that had characteristics of a small town. After visiting and measuring towns in Florida and throughout the South, they began to realize what an enormous opportunity the small town represented as a model to confront—in fact, to dismantle—some of the prevailing standards of typical residential developments.

Several years later, a plan and a code for Seaside, Florida emerged as an ingenious graphic formulation of the critique. Duany and Plater-Zyberk devised a method for radically reconfiguring the composition of the typical residential street and for replacing its ersatz formulas of making fabric and space with coherent guidelines for controlled incremental growth. These initial drawings, seen as diagrams, are perhaps the scheme's most important contribution (pp. 98–99).

*Comparative plans: University of
Virginia, "Elm Street" one-acre lots
and 1/4-acre lots*

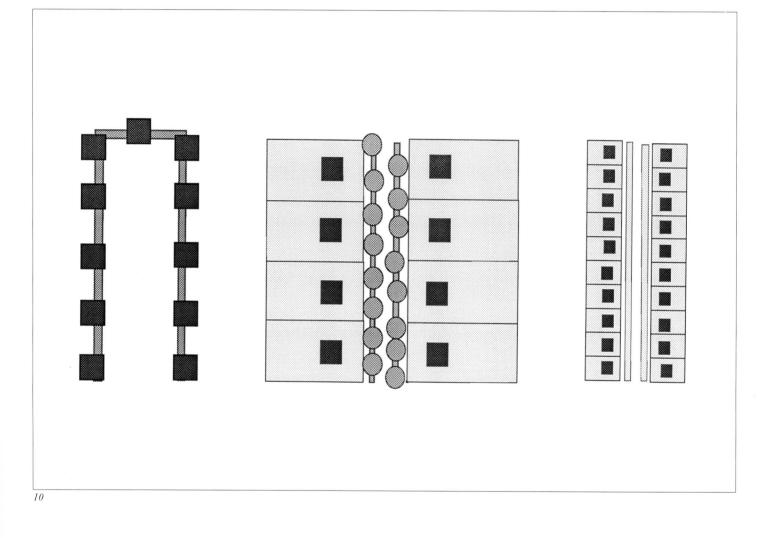

The Plan

Although most new residential developments pride themselves on exclusivity, the initial gestures of the Seaside plan reintroduce the public space of street and square as the basic matrix of the town. The Seaside plan straddles a two-lane shoreline highway that connects all the ocean-front communities, and, as in many Florida towns, serves as the main public thoroughfare and meeting ground.

The grid network, as modified by a radial and concentric organization, recalls various American hybrids of the City Beautiful and the Garden City such as John Nolen's own Mariemont, Ohio or Kingsport, Tennessee. As a central-square, oceanfront town, Seaside resembles New World towns like St. Augustine, Florida. As a resort community, the town has several important precedents in the state of Florida such as Coral Gables and Venice (fig. 12).

The New Residential Street

The post-World War II subdivision usually set out a limited hierarchy of streets: a large arterial and one type of residential street that was repeated throughout the development. The residential street was usually derived from the science of traffic engineering and worked independently from the houses that populated it. At Seaside, a hierarchy of streets and thoroughfares descends in size from the main street. From alleys to boulevards, each street is cast as a special kind of space according to its function and position within the town. The street hierarchy furthers the dialogue between public and private space by extending public territory from major streets into minor streets. At the same time the gradually decreasing size of roads creates more intimate areas in which to build a home and enjoy privacy. The flexible hierarchical network allows a variety of routes that filter traffic through the town better than a single large arterial.

The Urban Code

The Seaside urban code sets up an interdependency between road width, landscaping, lot size, and housing type. Regulation of the spatial modeling of the street is perhaps its most important function. For example, streets with back alleys or sideyards may have smaller roadways, smaller lots, and reduced setbacks. A larger boulevard may hold in the balance a greater setback, larger lots, and taller buildings. When a housing type requires a larger front lawn, the street section is defined by wooden fences, which are designed individually for each house. The fence system extends to form a kind of entry gate for each shore-front street, and its dimension defines the roadside parking area. Corner lots fronting the main road have larger setbacks, which in turn help to enclose a series of backyards and alleys.

The Architectural Code

The success of the street section is equally dependent on its buildings. These are controlled by an architectural code augments the urban code. Models for building classes, which accompany each street type, are based on southern vernacular housing from such places as Charleston and New Orleans' Vieux Carré.

A mandatory part of the architectural code is, for instance, the front porch found in most southern residential types. The porch is a pivotal element in the small town; it mediates between building and landscape and between the public and private realm by extending

*John Loretz Hancock included
interviews with several planners as an
appendix to his dissertation on John
Nolen. He posed the following question to Elbert Peets: "What is your
opinion of planning now and its future
as of now?" Elbert Peets replied:
"I think that planning is in ruin due
to unplastic legal regulations and the
failure to supply large area guidelines,
that is to determine types of streets and
roads appropriate to land use. We
need specialized streets permitting
residential housing to use smaller
streets and lots if they will etc. and if
the gross density is low the net density
can be high."[7]*

entry and visual penetration from the street. The architectural code also establishes window and massing proportions, a range of roof pitches, material restrictions, and some mandatory construction details. The details were intended to provide keys to proper building in a given material. (Code restrictions are lifted for the main public square and subsidiary public spaces within the neighborhoods.)

The architectural code, it naturally follows, is sugges-tive of a style of building. In its initial years of growth, the code has been interpreted within a housing market that mandates and trades on image.[8]

An emphasis on architectural image makes the town increasingly vulnerable to imitators attempting to market the "Seaside look." Without the more significant spatial dictates of the code and the plan diagram, Seaside would be the "neo-small town" condominium development that the entire scheme stands to critique. Unfortunately, most photographs of the town that are presented in the media provide more information about the architectural code than the urban code. And it is the urban code, in the end, which truly distinguishes Seaside.

There are ingredients in the master plan that are designed to inhibit some of the powers of the architectural code. Seaside is not an artificial environ-ment to be built overnight. The plan insists on incremental change and growth to be executed by a number of designers and contributors over time. The number of public buildings and their function, for instance, may change. The code will also be reinterpreted with the work of each new architect who works in the town. Each slightly deviant interpretation strengthens the critique proposed by the town and

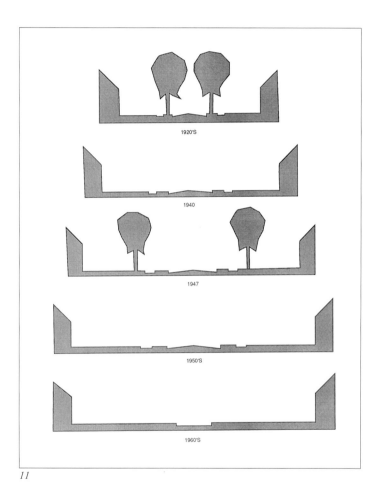

11

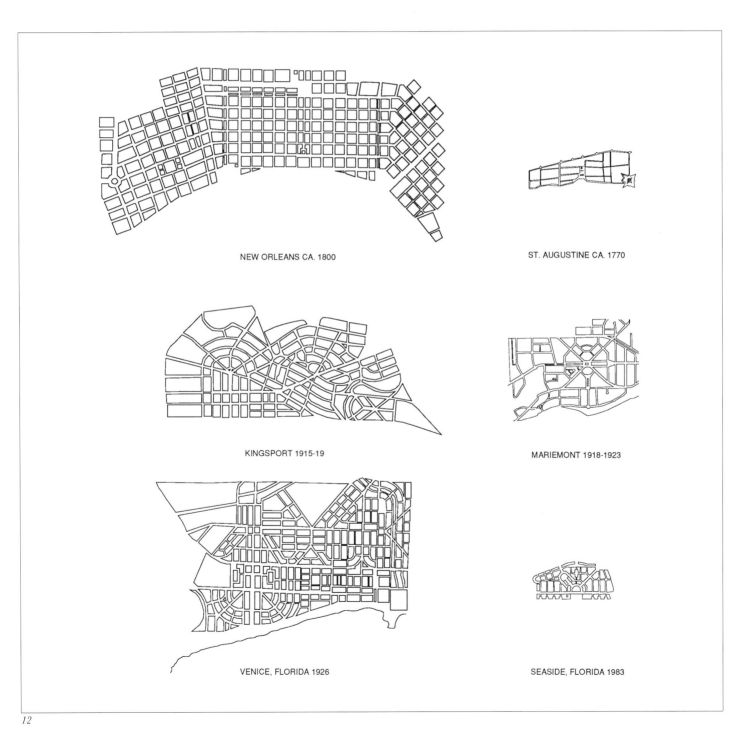

NEW ORLEANS CA. 1800

ST. AUGUSTINE CA. 1770

KINGSPORT 1915-19

MARIEMONT 1918-1923

VENICE, FLORIDA 1926

SEASIDE, FLORIDA 1983

12

13

14

makes Seaside a more elusive target for superficial market appraisal.

The Developer

Fortunately, Seaside's formula for growth is also economically feasible for the developer. In Seaside, the developer, with the help of experts, sets up a plan which then becomes a kind of public agreement among those who invest in the town's property. The developer, along with a representative of the design office, forms an authority to screen buildings for compliance to the code. The developer incurs less risk if he develops the subdivision gradually through lot sales than if he follows the standard practice of developing a subdivision all at once. Also, as he adds public amenities and controls the quality of the built environment, the developer increases the value of his land. In the initial stages of the development these amenities consist of well-designed spatial organizations, rather than more costly investments, such as golf courses or other recreational facilities, thus allowing the developer to maintain a low debt over the initial years of the town's growth. The large amount of public space that the developer provides works in tandem with increased densities. Such a promising solution results not only from sensitive motives and good design, but also from close cooperation between the public, the designer, and the developer, all of whom benefit from a long-term collaboration.

Small Scale Urbanism in a Regional Context

The words "town" and "suburb" are often used imprecisely. There are important distinctions to be made between various forms of settlement in America, and their precise appraisal is critical in understanding and altering our patterns of urban growth. What constitutes a town that fosters political process instead of private control and encourages citizenry rather than consumption?

Seaside calls itself a town. At eighty acres, its boundaries stand at the limits of comfortable walking distance and it is comparable in size to the neighborhood unit as it was formulated in the 1920s and 1930s. It is one-fifth the size of Mariemont, Ohio and less than half the size of Radburn, New Jersey.

Seaside is not large enough to be a municipality in the state of Florida and its form of self-governance will approximate that of many other homeowners' associations in America. The scheme for Seaside's additional centers of development (pp. 106–107) reflects an idea held by Andres Duany and Elizabeth Plater-Zyberk that a larger town should be made up of smaller neighborhood units because of the convenient walking distances that these neighborhoods define. As their practice receives commissions of larger and larger land areas, the Seaside idea is being applied, to some extent, as a prototype for neighborhoods within larger towns. Seaside deals with changes to suburban fabric and stops short of producing a critique concerning larger patterns of urban growth in America with regional, ecological, and political ramifications. There is certainly historical precedent in America for the small town as a means of identifying or organizing a region ecologically and politically. The courthouse town is one example. Regionalist planning of the twenties and thirties produced several working prototypes including Norris, Tennessee and the greenbelt towns. Peter Calthorpe's "pedestrian pockets" suggest the possibility of networks

13.
Sharecropper's cottage and
Leon Krier's house, Seaside
14.
Honeymoon cottages, Seaside
(Photos: Keller Easterling)

15.
Comparative sizes of suburban com-
munities in acres: dark tones indicate
developed land, light tones indicate
greenbelts

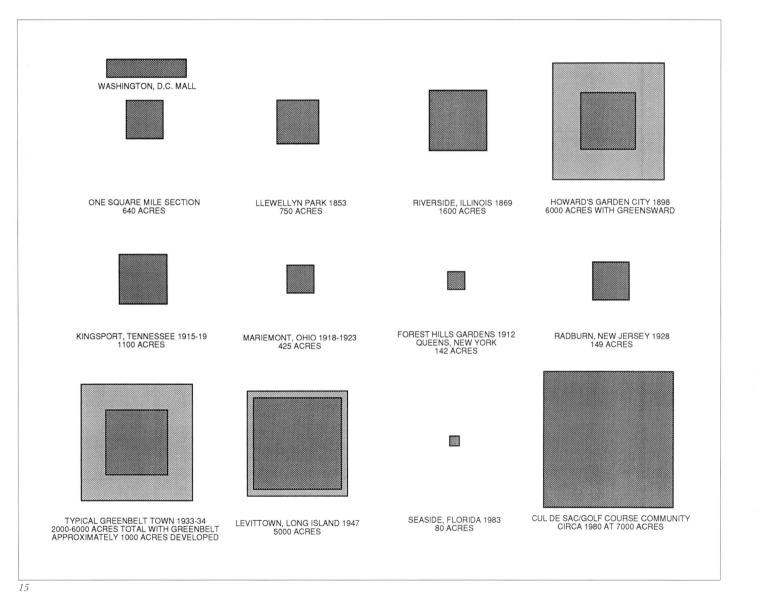

WASHINGTON, D.C. MALL

ONE SQUARE MILE SECTION
640 ACRES

LLEWELLYN PARK 1853
750 ACRES

RIVERSIDE, ILLINOIS 1869
1600 ACRES

HOWARD'S GARDEN CITY 1898
6000 ACRES WITH GREENSWARD

KINGSPORT, TENNESSEE 1915-19
1100 ACRES

MARIEMONT, OHIO 1918-1923
425 ACRES

FOREST HILLS GARDENS 1912
QUEENS, NEW YORK
142 ACRES

RADBURN, NEW JERSEY 1928
149 ACRES

TYPICAL GREENBELT TOWN 1933-34
2000-6000 ACRES TOTAL WITH GREENBELT
APPROXIMATELY 1000 ACRES DEVELOPED

LEVITTOWN, LONG ISLAND 1947
5000 ACRES

SEASIDE, FLORIDA 1983
80 ACRES

CUL DE SAC/GOLF COURSE COMMUNITY
CIRCA 1980 AT 7000 ACRES

15

of small-scale urbanism that respond to larger regional planning issues. Working at the Center for Rural Massachusetts in the Connecticut River Valley, Robert Yaro has proposed a means of controlling development in the landscape which has larger regional and land use implications.[9]

Seaside stands as the first stage of a thorough critique of our current methods of making communities. It establishes a fundamental precedent that reforms the design of the residential street as public space, it demonstrates the economic viability of the flexible, hierarchical grid network as an alternative to the typical streets and arteries of Briarhaven, and its plan for incremental growth also begins to encourage the notion of a "partnership"—a partnership of citizens rather than consumers.

The magic of the small town lies in its potential to create urban "jazz"—to allow for anarchy and variation within a rhythm and tune—to allow for deviance and counterpoint in those buildings that come together to maintain the line of a street and encourage a public eye. Already the town has established and overturned its normative taste to include more diversity. Over the years, Seaside will be all the richer for its revisions, its mirages, and its unpredictable additions.

*This essay is a revised version of the article "Public Enterprise,"
which first appeared in the Princeton Architectural Journal,*
Landscape, *vol. 2 (Princeton, NJ: Princeton Architectural
Press, 1985), 35–43.*

Notes

1.
John Nolen, ed. *City Planning* (New York and London: D. Appleton and Company, 1924), 35.

2.
Richard Louv, *America II* (New York: Penguin Books, 1985), xiii.

3.
Barker, Buono, Hildebrandt, eds., *The Small Town Design Book* (Mississippi: Mississippi State University, 1981), passim. Mississippi State University has devoted an entire division of its architecture program to the study of the small town as an art object. Students analyze the relationships between building and landscape and among objects in the built environment by finding narrative and musical analogies. They may build a method of analysis from a text of Eudora Welty or William Faulkner; the street may be seen as an orchestration, a "score" of events. Mississippi State University is one of the few schools to offer training that responds to issues regarding suburbia and small-scale urbanism.

4.
Michael Dennis, "Excursus Americanus," *Court and Garden: From the French Hotel to the City of Modern Architecture* (Cambridge, MA: MIT Press, 1986), 240.

5.
Ibid., 231.

6.
Ibid., 240.

7.
John Loretz Hancock, "John Nolen and the American City Planning Movement: A History of Cultural Change and Community Response 1900–1940," (Ph.D. dissertation, University of Pennsylvania, 1964), 621.

8.
Other historical prototype communities (Letchworth or Forest Hills Gardens, for example) have carried with them a slight disclaimer about their reliance on visual image to support what is really a spatial and ideological shift in design sensibility.

9.
Robert D. Yaro et al., *Dealing with Change in the Connecticut River Valley: A Design Manual for Conservation and Development* (Cambridge, MA: Lincoln Institute of Land Policy and the Environmental Law Foundation, 1989), passim.

David Mohney

Interview with Andres Duany

DM: How did you become involved with Seaside?

AD: Arquitectonica was recommended by Susan Lewin, who was then an editor of *House Beautiful*. Robert Davis, the developer, was designing with the architect who had done his last project, called Apogee, in Miami. That was a group of International Style town houses, very fine, especially for the time. They had done a sketch for what was to become Seaside, but there was no conception of it as a town (p. 88). There were some staggered housing clusters connected by boardwalks all over the site. Susan Lewin told Robert to look us up. Lizz and I were partners at Arquitectonica at the time; it was one of our projects within the firm. The original commission included only the central portion of the site with forty or fifty residential units and several commercial buildings. Our first scheme was that of a town but, in the fashion of Arquitectonica, it was as diagrammatic as possible: it had a four-square "downtown" intersection; inland "cabins" were distributed along a curving road, and an exhedra of "beach houses" faced the gulf (p. 89). There was already the idea of type differentiation by location rather than program: the size of the housing units might not vary, but those inland would be different from those on the beach. Nothing much happened with that plan.

Then at one point, I don't remember exactly when, Robert said, "Let's do the entire site." By that time, we were firmly convinced that it should be a real town.

DM: And that came about from . . .

AD: Reading. Like so many of our generation who had been taught urbanism in terms of Team X, we were confused about cities. Then, through his writings, Leon Krier showed us how a real city is made (Robert Stern's and John Massengale's suburban investigations

were important, too). That is why Krier is of such fundamental importance to us.

So we tried to conceive Seaside as a town. Even then, it was difficult to stop thinking in terms of conventional development practices. For example, our second attempt had the existing waterfront highway redirected around to the rear of the site, with a single controlled access point, the way conventional "pod" developments are entered. The problem with such a scheme was that the commercial component, normally the central focus of a town, had to be on the peripheral highway and therefore on the edge. The diagram didn't work at all: it could never be a town, but we disguised that by urban styling. Then we got off the boards, took a trip from Miami to the site in a big red convertible, and visited some of the little old Florida towns along the way. We found that they all straddled the major roads.

DM: Who's "we"?

AD: Daryl, Robert, and I. And when we arrived at the site, we said, "Hey! Let's not change the highway." It had the force of revelation, and many decisions quickly followed. Since it was going to be a wooden town with picket fences like the ones we had seen, the road system of the existing plan, which was circular, didn't work because wood fences cannot take curves. So it became a polygonal plan and Seaside emerged. (By this time, Lizz and I had left Arquitectonica, and Seaside was now our project.)

We continued to address the technical questions of how to make an American town since Krier's models were all European (they were the generation of La Villette). On this we worked separately. We photographed and sought out dimensions, and actually learned how to make a town. We observed the street of

1.
View from the beach across dunes
to Seaside
(Photo: David Mohney)

1

trees, the parking, the stores, the porches and so on.

DM: So you were studying existing precedents. Florida towns exclusively?

AD: Mostly Florida, for Lizz and me. Robert and Daryl did more traveling in Georgia and Alabama. We exchanged notes. Robert took the bulk of the slides. This took time, but there was a recession and Robert couldn't do much building anyway.

Now, the idea of having the buildings designed by many architects was ours. We were to be the architects for the whole project, and we could have done everything—it was our commission. But we realized that it would be dull to do so. A single firm cannot achieve authentic variety; only the work of many can achieve the character of a true town. So we decided to write a set of rules and invite lots of people to design. Years back, in 1977, we had done an urban design project at the University of Miami sited on the grounds of the naval base at Key West. We had designed a plan and had written a simple code from which students designed separate buildings, and it all worked. We have been interested in codes since. At the time, we didn't know how much we had to learn, to experiment to be able to do it. It seemed such a simple exercise then.

DM: When did you realize that the code might be the central facet to making the town?

AD: For us, from the beginning. For others, I think that it dawned as the town actually emerged. In the beginning, I sometimes had to defend the code: "Pay attention to the code, pay attention to the code, pay attention to the code." Now that it has proven to be a fairly reliable guarantee of quality, everybody is defending it furiously. It delivers quite respectable urban architecture without too much of a pain for the designer. By

the way, only a portion of the buildings at Seaside are by trained designers: a good number are by carpenters, drafting services, or by the owners themselves.

DM: How does the code fit into changing the idea of going beyond a development to making a town?

AD: The code is the tool that implements the town design in three dimensions, ensuring that its streets and squares are spatially defined and that the assignment of building types is respected during a build out which may well exceed the lifetime of the designers. By this time we had had the experience of building Charleston Place in Boca Raton (p. 45), which has 110 dwellings. It had fine streets, squares, parks, alleys, and walkways. But we had designed all the buildings, and it was not interesting to keep walking block after block the way it is at Seaside, because there was no authentic variety. It was all of the same architectural sensibility. Even we, the designers, were not interested in visiting all the blocks. We saw this as a flaw that historical towns do not suffer. It was our intention here to build a true town with a history beyond a single design campaign, and that could be done only over time by dozens of design personalities ordered by a code.

DM: How does the code work?

AD: A really good code takes care of the urban quality. The Seaside code creates urban qualities through the control of building type. Its primary concern is the making of the public realm through the definition of space. But there are other prescriptions with social implications: sideyards, location of parking, provision for porches or arcades, variations from one neighborhood to another, the encouragement of out-buildings, etc. And then there are elements that may be considered purely aesthetic, but that we believe to

2.
Driving piles for a house foundation
(Photo: David Mohney)
3.
Early version of the Seaside
Urban Code
4.
Outbuilding: a garage with a usable
second floor. This type of structure is
encouraged by the code.
(Photo: Michael Moran)

2

be essential to the urban quality. One is that roof pitches are specified within a certain range, and the other is that window proportions must be vertical or square. Towns considered beautiful are made of buildings which share an attitude towards the proportion of openings and towards roof type.

The code I have been describing we call the urban code. Together with the plan, it helps the town to exist socially and to be a viable organization. There is a second code, the architectural code, which forms the buildings by prescribing materials and methods of construction as we found it in the vernacular of the Gulf Coast. It is this second code that makes Seaside look as homogeneous as it does. It is the attempt, principally at Robert's urging, to make Seaside a well-built town architecturally, not only a well-working town socially, which was Lizz's and my interest.

DM: You sound as if you would dispense with the architectural code.

AD: Not now, although a couple of years ago I think we might have. We think that Robert was right. Besides, the developers of the other towns that we have designed expect a high level of architectural harmony. This has been a tradition since the 1920s in the U.S.

DM: What are the elements of it?

AD: The principal element of Seaside's architectural code is the limitation of materials to those generally in use prior to 1940. This is not an arbitrary date. Before the war, materials were what they were. Plywood was plywood, boards were boards, asphalt shingles were just that. Afterwards, industrially-derived ersatz was insinuated into the American building culture. Plywood is now shaped like tongue and groove, and petroleum derivatives are made to look like wood shakes and so

on. Apart from a personal dislike for these genetic monsters, they simply age badly. All materials age, but textured plywood, when old, looks like hell, while old board and batten has enough dignity to tempt people to recycle it as interior decoration. Also, the code has provisions for certain types of details, such as open rafter ends and certain minimum dimensions of joists and beams so that things don't look too flimsy. It keeps the buildings honest, and accounts for a high quality of construction. I think that the problem of Seaside being too cute comes not from the architectural code, which is pretty objective stuff, but from its interpretation by contemporary American consumer-clients.

DM: Describe the urban code in detail.

AD: The urban code prescribes eight different building types. We had clear, physical prototypes in mind, like Jackson Square and the Charleston "single house." Our code has a predictable three-dimensional result. Conventional codes are formulas that predict only quantities (floor to area ratio, for example). Conventional codes end up being hundreds of pages long; the Seaside urban code is one page. We devised its particular format by testing it with students at the University of Miami. The students were given the code, and would deliver it dependably, never having seen the intended prototype.

It is interesting to compare the Seaside code with Christopher Alexander's "pattern language." We agree with the town that he proposes. He knows what he is talking about as an end, but he is too idealistic about implementation. You must be intelligent and literate, and have a good deal of time, to read Alexander's book, which is the instrument of implementation. But you can build your part of Seaside without understand-

3

4

Following pages
5.
View towards beach, including
Deborah Berke's Averett Tower and
House and Ernesto Buch's Tupelo
Street Beach Pavilion
(Photo: David Mohney)
6.
Streetscape showing similarities in roof
pitch and materials
7–8.
Picket fences
(Photos: Michael Moran)

ing any of the principles because we use a code, not a book. Designers are accustomed to following codes in this country, which is fortunate because they hardly know anything about making urbanism. Their buildings do not make towns. So if we and Alexander are after the same town, we are more practical about it. We count on codes having a much greater impact in salvaging American urbanism than books ever could.

DM: Let's talk for a minute about the prototypes: did you have preconceptions about them? Did you think that only existing types would work, or did the possibility exist that there could be invented prototypes?

AD: Of course you can innovate, but we are suspicious of invention. Urbanists have spent the last fifty years inventing prototypes and the resulting agglomerations— "towns" or "cities" is too flattering a term—have been trash. Traditional buildings are an inexhaustible lode of wisdom about society, climate, and construction. A designer who participates in the vernacular tradition starts so far ahead of an invention-prone colleague, that it is no contest. It's okay and even laudable to experiment with a single private house, but it's irresponsible to risk an entire community and the happiness of its future citizens with untested invention. The traditional types that we used fell cleanly into place, because there was an empirical logic to their selection. Type I forms the downtown commercial square with arcaded party-wall buildings three- to five-stories-tall (pp. 101–103). Type II is also a party-wall type, which is used at the town hall square. It is highly controlled, in a New Orleans way, with the cornices and balconies all lined up to be suitable for a dignified civic space. Type III is for the mixed-use district immediately behind it. It is a party-wall building type that delivers

three-story town houses or workshops. These three make up the continuous fabric of the downtown. They are fundamental types. The manipulation of variables gives practically any downtown building type except the high rise. With them, you have the American town, but not the American city, which would require the high rise.

Then there are the freestanding houses selected from the range available in the South. Type IV is the large freestanding structure, which we call the "antebellum mansion," and which Ungers calls the "urban villa." It is a type that doesn't exist in modern zoning codes, which is too bad, because it is very flexible and useful. It can be a single-family house, a duplex, a small apartment building with four or six units, an inn, or a professional office. It is a transitional building that allows varying the proportion of commercial to residential over the long term. Old towns that have a stock of this type are fortunate indeed. Type VI is the "bungalow," with the second story within the roof pitch and a lot of porch. It is the bread and butter of the rural South, and it is the primary "suburban" type of Seaside. Type VII is the "sideyard single house" of Charleston. Type VIII is a full two stories with small yards on the sides. There are other types in the South, of course: the "camelback," the "dogtrot" and the "shotgun," for example. These too could have been achieved by manipulating the variables of the code. But we didn't think that they were as useful as, say, the "bungalow" and the "single house," which provide fundamental urban choices because one of them involves a front yard and the other a sideyard. One gives a swath of space to the street, while the other is tight to the street, and secures a great deal of privacy for the yard. We

65

5

6

felt no obligation to use all of the South's building types. A town does not need to be a typological supermarket.

DM: And how did you use each of these types in regard to the Seaside plan?

AD: An example: The north-south streets, which end on the ocean, are coded Type VI, with large front yards (i.e. big setbacks from the street) to make the view corridor wide. The east-west streets, which don't have an important view at the terminus, are generally Type VII sideyard houses which are close to the street. In testing with students we discovered that the code was so efficient that there wasn't enough variety, so we developed the Type VIII, which is more liberal in its prescription. This type is sprinkled as a leavening device in special places, where urban intensity is desirable. They are used at the squares and, in some places, a pair will provide a kind of gateway.
Now, back to Type V, which I skipped over. Our code is based on the making of public space; the datum is the streetline. Everything is fixed on the street. This means that coding is difficult on certain lots, which, due to geographic circumstance, are more than one building deep. Where these occur at the eastern boundary and south of Route 30–A, they are assigned the Type V. They are the equivalent of the old bungalow courts where a single architect designed all the houses and resolved the internal site planning simultaneously. Rosewalk is one of these special neighborhoods.
We tested the code with students not only to achieve precision in compliance with the prototype, but also to avoid precluding good ideas. If someone had a valid idea, we adjusted the code to allow it. Roof decks and towers were the result of these adjustments.

DM: And there is a provision for towers in the code?
AD: There is a provision in the code stating that one can build, without height restriction, a structure with a footprint less than 215 square feet. That generates a tower slim enough to avoid blocking someone else's view. By allowing towers, everyone, even the most landlocked, has a shot at the ocean view. The towers, in fact, will be very significant to the image of Seaside. Charleston has the sideyard house which immediately identifies the city; it seems that Seaside is going to be a city of towers, unlike any other I know of in America.
DM: How is the code supervised?
AD: By the Town Architect. This position is usually held by a young architect or student who lives at Seaside. There have been six so far: Ernesto Buch, Teofilo Victoria, Derrick Smith, Tom Christ, John Massengale, and Victoria Casasco. They review the designs for compliance with the code. To help them, we have instituted certain bureaucratic symbols, like application forms and an approval stamp. We found that to administer rules, there is a certain need for authority which only a bureaucracy and its procedures can fill. It took us a while to realize the need for formalized procedures to gain respect for the code. Because Robert Davis is so accessible and such a nice person temperamentally, he would be faced with comments like, "Hey, Robert, I added an extra two feet on the balcony. I hope you don't mind!" Now the plans go through a deliberate process that takes time, and acquire a stamp at the end. There is something impersonal about authority which is crucial; it would be even better if the Town Architect were housed in a dignified building. At the moment it's not particularly respectable where you go to get permits; it's too home-style.

7

8

DM: Do you or Lizz ever have a hand in personally supervising the code?

AD: Almost never. Robert calls us when something unforeseen slips by. If it is destructive to the urbanism or the architectural vernacular, we adjust the codes to preclude it in the future.

DM: So your actual participation is limited to setting out the urban plan, writing the codes, and then you very consciously removed yourself from any further deliberations. It is rare to see architects walk away from buildings, but that's the experiment, isn't it?

AD: The experiment is to have clean hands, so to speak, to show that the code works technically, without the influence of our buildings. From time to time Robert does involve us if there is trouble with an architect and we try to mediate. But the architects involved hate it, so we try to stay clear of it, unless we can say something positive. But there are times when we think that we will do a building here.

DM: Why the change?

AD: Because I think that already it is becoming clear that the code does its job, that we don't control it in some way. And the building that we might do is our own place. It still might not happen, because it's not clear to me that we should do it.

DM: At this stage, or . . .

AD: At this stage, or at any stage. I have one instinct as an architect who wants to live in his own work, and another that we should be completely clear of this now—the issue is very fudged. Furthermore, the issue is very unclear in the press regarding what we have done and what anybody else has done. It is very unclear that we haven't done all the buildings. Sometimes it is unclear that the buildings exist. People just

don't understand that, and to do a building might fudge that even more.

DM: Do you allow variances to the code?

AD: The code says simply, "Variances are granted on the basis of architectural merit." It was one of the adjustments made to avoid preventing what was good. But what is curious is that almost no one has asked for a variance. In fact, I only know of one person who has asked for a variance, and that was the architect who designed the house at the top of Tupelo Street with the cupola; it has a higher roof pitch than permitted. He was one of the first buyers at Seaside, and he bought before the code existed. His argument was that he didn't know that he was buying a place that was coded.

DM: That house is very prominent as you look up Tupelo Street.

AD: What the typical house should do is homogenize the fabric, and assign a proper hierarchy to public and private buildings. That house breaks the public/private relationship, violates it thoroughly. It looks like a public building, both in its siting, and its architectural configuration. It will be less prominent once the rest of the buildings around it are done; they are Type VIII's, and tend to be more liberal in their configuration.

DM: Have you had to make other adjustments?

AD: There were slight adjustments. Here's one: historical Charleston sideyard houses have zero setback on one side. We found that the fire code did not permit windows on the zero setback side, so we had to specify a five-foot easement on that side. The type is physically the same and the fire marshal is happy. Another example: originally fences were not required at the rear walkways and as a result, the public/private definition at the rear yards was ambiguous.

9.
Type VI house
(Photo: David Mohney)

9

The code isn't the only variable; lot size is also manipulated. For example, the provisions of the Type VI are applied to forty-, fifty-, and sixty-foot lot widths. The design of the lot dimensions is a substantial urban design tool. If we do not design the lots, we cannot code with any refinement. We need to be able to make larger corner lots and smaller town center lots.

The problem with urban planning as it is currently practiced in the suburbs is that land is platted and sold in "pods." These are large amorphous tracts containing dozens of buildings. No determined physical result is possible with such a crude planning tool. Spatial definition occurs only by accident and a coherent urbanism is virtually impossible.

DM: I think what you are saying is that you couldn't take on the existing Seaside code and apply it to any existing plat in another community . . .

AD: Exactly, the plan has to be designed together with the code. Of course, Seaside is at the maximum of refinement; you could design a more crude urbanism and it would still work. After all, there are traditional neighborhoods with only one type of lot, and they aren't bad.

DM: Just for the record, could you give a brief comparison of the way that the code differentiates between Type IV, the "antebellum mansion," and Type VI, the "bungalow."

AD: Type IV is a large lot with substantial front, rear and side setbacks, and the building envelope is centered. Type VI is smaller all the way around and has a larger setback on one side than the other. The small side is for services; the large setback inflects the best yard toward the ocean.

DM: It is as if a little bit of the Charleston "single house" is creeping in.

AD: Almost any building will improve with the loading to a sideyard. A refinement in urbanism that should be more widespread is the asymmetrical sideyard. It can inflect a town toward the better solar orientation, and put the service side in a place that neighboring designers can count on. Anyway, the Type IV setbacks are not inflected, because they are on a grand avenue inland, away from the view. Type IV requires a two-story porch which extends along 100 percent of the front facade, while Type VI requires only 35 percent of the front to be porch. Type IV therefore forms a grand single composition, worthy of the avenue. Type VI is only 11/2 stories, while Type IV is two full stories. In both types, the rear yard is very large; outbuildings are thereby encouraged as the only way to fully build out the site. The permitted parking location is similar for both, generally to the side or rear of the lot. Wherever a parking place coincides with an outbuilding, a garage may occur. The garages will always be outbuildings, in that wise pre-war tradition that secures privacy for the rear yards. And so the types come into being.

DM: Talk about the picket fences.

AD: We found, generally speaking, American towns have a street space (building face to building face) that is wider than European street space. For example, Paris has a proportion of street width to building height of 1:1.5. Italian streets often have an even higher proportion; it might be 1:2 or 1:3, like Florence. American towns may have a street space of 6:1 or 10:1, which is basically unsatisfactory, since it is beyond the proportion that makes defined space perceivable. But then two amending factors come into play: one is the steady rows of trees ("Elm Street"), which corrects the excessively wide proportion. The second element

10

with space defining characteristics is the fence. The fences are there not to be cute or nostalgic, and not only for territorial definition, but for spatial definition. There is a provision in the code that every fence must be different. This has the effect that everyone must expend a substantial amount of creativity on the design of their fence. It seems to absorb that instinct for customizing that is otherwise asserted by elaborate carriage lamps, fake shutters, and the like.

DM: Let me ask you one question about Type V, the Special Neighborhood type. Looking carefully at the Type V houses at Rosewalk over the last couple of days as well as on the previous trip, I find myself feeling uncomfortable with them. It is not a feeling that derives from the architectural basis of the houses; it is clear that the people who worked on them are quite capable architects. But elsewhere, there is a variety that exists house to house, which is not so evident in the houses that comprise Rosewalk. Do you see that? Is that an issue for you when you think about the code?

AD: Frankly, I was hoping that the Type V would generate less variety than it does, that it would generate that kind of set piece on the order of the meeting ground at Martha's Vineyard, the perfect little houses, or of the cabins at the Neshoba Country Fair. I was really hoping that there would be an aligning of the buildings as at the University of Virginia (although there is some variety building to building), in a very homogeneous way, or, like the Aldo Rossi beach house, an extremely repetitive type. Rosewalk, like all Type V sites, is designed by a single firm. It is intended to be a completely coherent enclave with whatever special beauty ensues from that. We were expecting that there would occur a bungalow court on formal

lines. But as it turned out, Rosewalk buildings did the opposite: there is much more variety in massing, and a picturesque organization, so I think that the opportunity was lost. You should know that the original site design by Orr and Taylor was steadier, but it was altered to save existing vegetation. Architecturally, Rosewalk is quite Victorian, which turned out to be very popular, and it was influential throughout Seaside.

DM: Is there a differential at work between the image you have of Seaside and what is being built?

AD: Yes. The town has a history of its own, which may be compressed, but is nevertheless authentic. Seaside has evolved through many hands, Robert Davis's most important among them, and it is all the better for it. It is a much more interesting place than I thought it would be.

DM: A question of style and urbanism: at the symposium on Seaside in New York, Deborah Berke and Robert Stern had an exchange based on Bob's assertion that it is impossible to have urbanism without a singular style, and her uncomfortable reaction to that. Her point was that the aims of architecture over the last two centuries are antithetical to that idea; that making architecture today is not an exercise disposed toward a previous style.

AD: Toward a previous style or a singular style?

DM: Maybe it is both questions.

AD: I think I can answer both. First, there are certain styles that have indeed lost their validity. But there are certain other styles, generally those derived from a system of construction, that continue to make sense. We were conscious of this in proposing the particular vernacular that is used at Seaside, which is the Southern version of balloon-frame construction. It is the best way to

11

build in this climate: wood frame and wood skin; it is the most sensible and expressive way and it is not pegged in time. A house like the one we are in could have been built from the 1880s to the 1940s, even into the 1960s in some areas. By selecting a valid construction technique, we inevitably selected a valid style. If somebody were to ask for Old English or French Empire, we would be incapable of coding that, because those are archaic styles without continued technical validity.

DM: So what you are saying is that there is room for invention within some aspects of the way this is put together; there is room for history, and aesthetic precedents, but still room for invention . . .

AD: Yes, but not just that. This architecture is based on valid construction techniques, and thus has a permanent authority, unlike those based on independent aesthetics that pass as fashions pass.

DM: You mentioned earlier some of the things in the architectural code that you thought you could do away with, that were secondary . . .

AD: That's another question. Coherent urbanism does not require a single coherent style. You can have a city or a town which has Georgian buildings next to Richardsonian buildings next to postmodern buildings. Such towns exist and work well; Savannah is one. The minimum discipline of urbanism is the existence of agreements regarding setbacks and building heights in order to make coherent public space. But to make a town harmonious also requires a narrowing of the architectural possibilities. Any town that is good looking enough to appear on a travel poster has a limited range of architectural elements. Charleston is one of these towns, Nantucket is another, and Seaside has that ambition. Robert Davis is tremendously ambitious

about this place. He wants all the refinements, and in the end it will be a poster-quality town. Now, that might be pretty deadly to some people. John Massengale once said, "You know, Seaside is very beautiful, but I have to go to Seagrove once in a while to breathe." [Seagrove is the adjacent town.]

DM: What is your own personal reaction to that level of refinement? Are you comfortable with Robert taking the project to that incredibly detailed level, or would you be willing to loosen it up?

AD: We are willing to loosen it up if we must, as we have in other projects; but we are equally interested in tightening up. We are very intrigued by eighteenth-century urbanism: street after street of completely steady cornice lines, and very slight variations. It can be very beautiful. Much of what is best in Rossi's work has to do with the beauty of repetition. Seaside doesn't have enough repetition. I admire certain descriptions of Greek ruins; seductive statements of "quiet grandeur" and "majestic simplicity," and Seaside doesn't have that.

DM: What is your creative relationship with the developer? Is Seaside a special circumstance?

AD: It is a very well-balanced circumstance, and we would hope to achieve it again, because it couldn't be better. There are certain historical analogies for this relationship: the Duke and the Minister; the Duke has the power and connoisseurship to implement the Minister's proposals. We consult by telephone at a healthy level of abstraction and then come up here once in a while. Robert, in big decisions and changes, consults with us. Ours is not the only advice he considers, but we triumph often enough. The unique aspect of Seaside, which cannot be a model for all other projects, is that Robert is so educated about

12

design that he can make many decisions himself.

DM: That allows you the distance a Minister needs?

AD: Yes. In other projects, I think we will have to be more constantly involved.

DM: Are you comfortable working for developers?

AD: Usually. But we are not comfortable with developers who have been ruined by mediocre architects. Many developers have been convinced by their designers or their periodicals that design is a checklist of tricks: wow them with the view as you open the front door; give them a bathroom that is nothing less than erotic; add skylights and redwood trim everywhere. This is what the developers cynically call "sizzle," as in "give them the sizzle and not the steak." Developers of this kind expect us to fulfill their checklist and we don't. We propose instead to provide meat and potatoes. Developers aren't dumb and we have generally been able to convince them. Then again, the problem may not always be the developer but that portion of the public that has been conditioned to expect sizzle. We don't know what makes them so gullible, whether it is Madison Avenue, Disney World, the good economic times, or some other force. They expect a very high degree of cute, they have no taste whatsoever for "quiet simplicity or majestic grandeur," but prefer pretty, perky, happy architecture. We personally find sweet buildings difficult to provide because we don't sympathize with the self-indulgent society that loves them so. Seaside is by no means free of that, and it should be made clear that the code does not enforce cute buildings (look at Robert Davis's own two houses or Steve Holl's building), but it does allow the owners to exercise their preference for them. Somebody once said, I think it was Pat Pinnell, that we had

designed Kansas, but were building Oz.

Going back to developers: they are the best kind of clients, because they have a great deal of power over place, power equivalent to that of the autocracies of the past, which formed great cities such as Paris, Rome, and Karlsruhe. Even in America, there were autocracies when it came to city design: William Penn decreed Philadelphia's plan and code, Ogelthorpe imposed Savannah, and Nicholson laid out Williamsburg and Annapolis. These plans weren't done by committee; they weren't presented to a neighborhood association—there was no plebiscite. History shows that you have to concentrate power to achieve decisive physical form, and developers are the people who currently hold such power in the United States.

You cannot today present an urban plan to a city council or a neighborhood association and expect it to survive as a strong idea, because the many voices will make it a morass. Given the current situation, developers are the remaining hope for urbanism. They have very large tracts of land under their unified power: it is not unusual to have six hundred or one thousand acres under one ownership, which is ten times the size of Seaside. There are dozens of tracts this size laid out every year, all of them potentially towns. That they are not is only because designers don't know how. The power is there, the land is there, and the market is there, but the designers are not there. So they deliver shopping centers, office parks, and housing clusters instead of towns: the undifferentiated suburbia which is destroying our society.

DM: Is Seaside already an alternative to this?

AD: Yes. We have been called to do it again in the past year, a dozen times. But we haven't been able to design many of these, because the roads had been laid out in such a way that it was impossible to design a town. It was too late; we couldn't accept the work.

DM: That means that the plans were dimensioned to a point that they couldn't be adapted . . .

AD: Yes. Spaghetti-like roads were platted and housing pods were approved as separate clusters. It was impossible within those parameters to correct the urban form.

DM: Are there mistakes you acknowledge at Seaside?

AD: Yes. There are technical errors. One of them is that some streets aren't wide enough, because people don't park with as much precision as we had thought. Also, I think the variety of colors works against a harmonious urbanism. The irony is that we wanted a good deal of variety, so the code banned brown and beige, the easy colors that everybody would automatically paint. This catalyzed the stupendous variety. Actually, many of these buildings are quite tough, and it is only the pretty colors that make them seem unreal. However, the colors have helped the marketing quite a lot; as I said, eighties Americans like pretty things. Then there are some things that are just omissions. For example, the lots on Route 30–A were to have 24-foot instead of the 16-foot front setbacks; this was not implemented through an oversight. There is a good bit of that sort of error, which is not all bad since it gives character to the place. We are torn between wanting the perfection embodied in the plan and code, and the exceptions that give so much character. Actually, there are so many buildings that follow the code exactly that Seaside can admit errors. For example, I don't know why Deborah Berke's house on Savannah Street seems to be a Type VII instead of a Type VI as coded, but it is just fine. And I love the beach pavilion on Tupelo Street, which does not line up properly with the axis of the street, thanks to a surveying error.

The greatest unexpected piece is the "temporary" restaurant downtown, which began with two cottages and has been extended sequentially by some ten designers, becoming a building with real history. It is interesting architecture, but lousy urbanism since a building that large really shouldn't be at that location. They were to be small structures to be used only until the downtown was built. But with the unexpected success of the restaurant, the building has expanded and become very solid. It is no longer the airy pavilion on the beach acting as a foil to the solid building edge of the town square. Leon considers that a bad thing: it is going to interfere with his tower.

DM: In terms of town planning, do you consider Seaside to be a success?

AD: It has become more successful than anybody thought it could be. It is more interesting architecturally; it is better known, and selling for more, too. Above all, it works better socially than we imagined any new architecture could, since the conventional wisdom of the last thirty years has been that social intentions and architecture do not mix well. The only significant failure is that it is not a town with a real variety of incomes. Because it became very desirable, only relatively well-off people buy here now.

DM: Is it fair to wait for the missing downtown before calling the town a complete success?

AD: It is only a residential neighborhood now and will not be a complete town until the downtown commercial section is done. Until the Type I, II, and III buildings are built, half the ingredients aren't in yet. Then we will see if there is indeed a whole. I have no doubts.

13

14

DM: Are you glad to be here, to visit?

AD: I find it very interesting to be here, because it is ongoing—that thrill a project in construction always affords its designer is endlessly prolonged here. It might be as long as ten years that this ecstasy—which in a building is usually compressed into the twelve months it takes to put footings on the ground, enclose the major space, put the roof on, and paint—continues to give you big thrills.

DM: And some are completely unexpected . . .

AD: The best part is that they are completely unexpected. And the strange thing is that very seldom have they been unpleasant surprises. Almost always they have been pleasant, because there are a lot of different minds at work on tiny little details, and little things that no single designer really has the scope of working out, of worrying about. And it is such a pleasure to see the care that so many minds and hands have applied to this. That is very valuable, because there is absolutely no way that a single designer—apart from the issues of authentic variety and so forth—could put as much thought and care into all those little pieces.

DM: Unless they were all the same.

AD: Yes. And even then, it is hard to imagine. Seaside, for a project so large, is rewarding on a very small scale. Our other projects (for example, Charleston Place for which we designed all the buildings) are rewarding at the scale of the urban space, but not at the scale of the details, which are repetitive. Seaside has the urban scale and also the details. It is great to visit here; it's like Christmas. You say, "What? Only five new houses this time?" You expect big thrills each time. Do you know how many planned towns have actually been completely built according to their plans? Almost none. Some have beautiful streets in place. John Nolen designed many in the twenties, but the buildings, mostly done in the fifties and sixties, are not responsive to the three-dimensional implications of the plan, and the town has not emerged. Nolen counted on the competence of architects to behave in an urbanistically responsible way, which was a good bet in the twenties, but the odds had changed by the fifties. His towns, with the exception of Mariemont, which was built out before the crash, are failures because he did not have strong codes. That is the principal difference between us and the planners of the twenties: we assume the incompetence or ill will of the designers and code accordingly. So we are confident about this one; if Robert survives whatever recession is coming, Seaside might be completed as planned, which would be unique. There is another problem: Robert and I have spent some time thinking about this. What happens fifty years down the line if some of the neighborhoods have deteriorated, and developers move in? All over Florida, the beautiful mansions along the shore are being demolished to make high rises. What is going to prevent that from happening here? We are thinking about certain legal instruments that might be established to allow the people on the north of Route 30–A to outvote the people to the front. Unfortunately, the power of money is such that a developer building on the shoreline can buy out the inland people. So the long range fate remains to be seen. There is a difference between completing a fine town and having the town survive deep into history. I suspect the odds are against it.

DM: So we'll see. Maybe you and I can come back in fifty years and take a look at it.

AD: I think we will be able to tell in ten.

David Mohney

Interview with Elizabeth Plater-Zyberk

DM: Three years ago, in the first interview, Andres noted that there wasn't enough repetition in the buildings at Seaside. Recent buildings seem to have even less repetition. Has the status of the architectural code changed since we talked three years ago? The question is asked in the context of the difference between the houses on Tupelo Street (built up largely from 1984–1986) which seem to be closer to the prototypical fabric buildings envisioned in the urban code, and Pensacola Street (constructed largely within the last year), with much larger, more individualistic structures.

EPZ: Do you mean has the code changed, or has its perception in the eyes of designers changed?

DM: I think it is both questions.

EPZ: The code hasn't changed. There has been some minor tinkering with it, but basically it is the same code.

DM: What about its status? How do individual designers look at it when they work at Seaside?

EPZ: I don't think more recent designs are responding to the code differently as much as they are responding to buildings that are already there. A substantial number of basic prototypical buildings has been constructed already. Some people don't want to repeat a good basic building. It doesn't represent the opportunity for design expression that a reinterpretation of the code does. A couple of people have tried to push it: Walter Chatham's own house, and Victoria Casasco's house (which I think are actually quite interesting buildings, and I like them) are definitely conscious retakes of the code, or reinterpretations of it, but certainly within the rules of the code.

DM: I also wonder if you can put it in economical terms as well: the people who bought at Seaside initially and paid a few thousand dollars for a lot could perhaps only afford a few thousand more dollars for a house. Now, to be able to buy land at Seaside, it takes tens of thousands of dollars, and you probably have to have tens or even hundreds of thousands of dollars available for a house.

EPZ: I don't think the elaboration of design is related to the availability of funds. I've never experienced people having more leeway for design with a larger budget; that's so rare. They usually want more space, not more design.

But I think the economic issue that is at play here is that since the land is more expensive, people are building out to the maximum volume; they are building as much as they can. It goes hand in hand with the rise in land prices. You see it in cities retrofitting, too, where the design corollary to the economic pressure is: the greater the bulk, the greater the creativity implied in dealing with that bulk. A small simple house is a different story than a large house with a complex program. So I think that is how the economics are affecting it, rather than that there is more money for design.

DM: Do you have an opinion about which are more successful? Are the smaller simpler houses more successful in an urban context?

EPZ: I don't think I could qualify it that way. One thing that is interesting is that the larger homes are in the correct gradation toward the town center, and that was the intention of the code, the placement of the types in that onionskin arrangement. I think people probably hanker for the simpler rendering of any idea, but no one expected people would be building out to allowable bulk as much as they have, that inflation of land prices leading to building bulk would happen so

15

16

immediately. But I think it is well within the realm of control. I don't think it is excessive. After all, a part of our theory is that a certain density of people is required to make a town walkable and to allow a town to provide the services to make it walkable.

DM: In the last three to four years, you have been involved to a great extent in writing urban codes for towns across America. Have you learned things in that process that you would apply to the Seaside code now? If you were to write the Seaside code today, how would it differ from ten years ago, when the whole process began?

EPZ: I have to think about that . . . . My first response to that is that the Seaside code has proven to be remarkably durable, and I think well thought out. We've had a lot of good criticism of it along the way, and we've explored changes in tinkering with it for Seaside, and we generally come back to making the changes pretty minimal. The one issue that is related to it, that comes to mind, however, which we did not anticipate at Seaside (and this is not a code issue), is that it would grow in value so quickly that the character of the town as a whole became different than was initially expected. Affordability and a mix of people, which were among the original design intentions, became an issue that we couldn't control as much as we expected. However, as building closes in on the downtown, we will be able to better judge whether one can design to provide for a range of incomes and types of people, i.e. in the workshop area, and the apartments above the shops, as well as the outbuildings. This layer, the Type III structures in the urban code, behind downtown has not occurred yet, which should scale down values, or at least maintain them.

One of the things we have learned, especially in the more urban projects we have worked on, is that there is a difference between design and policy; but they need to go hand in hand, too. Maintaining a mix of people or of commerce doesn't always happen by itself. At some point there has to be some sort of implementation policy to support your insistence on a range of people and on a certain serviceability of the retail. A developer or the municipality has to come to terms with this. This is one thing we were not thinking about at the time that has become very clear to us since then. Surprisingly or not, the part of that dual aspect that we can control, the design, rather than the policy, seems to withstand the test in the Seaside code.

DM: Parenthetically, I would add that I think Seaside is victimized, to some extent, by its success. The fact that there isn't any other thing like it, that it is unique, creates a hothouse atmosphere that inflates land values. If it does become something that can be repeated, I expect a much more rational development process to ensue.

EPZ: Absolutely. The answer to that problem is making more great places. You see that in a place like Miami where there is only one great place to go, like Coconut Grove, it overheats. It is going through a Jane Jacobs phase right now, in which it would seem to be about to destroy itself.

DM: Right: a New Yorker might call it the Columbus Avenue syndrome.

EPZ: Maybe New York is a better example, because New York has so many great places that heat up and cool down. That is probably the natural evolution of a place according to the American standard of land speculation, and the best thing you can do with a town

Preceding page
15.
One of the first buildings at Seaside,
this sharecropper's shack, which was
found abandoned along U.S. 98, was
moved to the town. It has been used
for a variety of purposes, most notably
as a take-out restaurant known locally
as the "shrimp shack."
(Photo: Duany/Plater-Zyberk)
16.
The market and restaurant, circa
1989. This assemblage has been
revised on an almost yearly basis.
(Photo: David Mohney)

This page
17.
Aerial view showing the relationships
between the north-south streets and the
beach pavilions.
(Photo: Duany/Plater-Zyberk)

17

or city plan is to make it flexible enough that it might accommodate that over many years, which brings us back to the grid.

DM: Have people actively tried to subvert the urban code at Seaside? Not in small ways, but big ones.

EPZ: I can't think of any. I think that some people may think that the Steve Holl building is a backfiring of the code rather than a good example of it. A lot of lay people feel that it is an ill-placed building, that it is actually in opposition to the character of the rest of Seaside. They see it as a contrasting and jarring element. I can understand that people perceive it to be that way now, but when it is accompanied by others of similar bulk and its party wall has a building attached, it is going to be a very different situation. No, I don't think there have been any major subversions. I guess maybe Tony Ames's project was pretty blatant in his intent. But we, in our response to his design, and the architectural review board, tried very hard to make it work by saying things like, "Let's make the flat roofs all decks," and things like that, to make his expression possible within the code. It didn't go ahead for other reasons.

DM: How important is the writing of urban codes to the process of development in America today, and is it the same situation for urban and rural areas?

EPZ: It is important because the codes are there, and they have been determining our urbanism for years, even though it may not seem important for those architects who simply respond to the existing codes. Codes are a horrifying, but significant, device for controlling design in this country, and codes are generally unconscious of their effect. They are trying to keep things from being too bad, but they have outlived their useful-

ness in the form in which they are now, and people are only beginning to realize this. If what we are proposing seems revolutionary to some people, it is only because we have been stuck with the other codes without reviewing them for too long. There should be a constant process of evolving controls; it is difficult to do something now that will last for 25 years—although the original Williamsburg code, for instance, is still valid.

DM: Your practice seems to be much more involved with urban design and writing codes than with architecture, at least compared to your work from five years ago. Is this a conscious choice you have made because you feel that there is an opportunity to do more in that manner?

EPZ: The demand for town planning has increased in the last two years, and we have responded in kind, by doing as much as we could. If the same thing happened with buildings, we would have done the same. But our willingness to strike out in this direction is fueled of course by the encouragement we have had from so many different quarters. It is true that we are now involved in more urban design than architecture, but we don't want to abandon architecture. We think it is very important that city planning, town planning, and urban design be done by architects. It is all too easy to blame non-architects for urban design problems while shrinking from that responsibility oneself. We have been extremely gratified and encouraged by the responses to our work, from lay people to planners to developers to elected officials. The fact that we've hit such a cross-grain response has made it seem that we are really filling a need, and with such an opportunity before us, that we should contribute as much as we can while the time seems right.

DM: In that context, then, let me ask this. Quite a large number of people have designed buildings at Seaside over the last six years; do you have any regrets at this point that you have not designed any buildings there yourselves?

EPZ: I don't. Part of the reason is that there has been so much architectural creativity there, that in fact if one or two people hadn't done their thing there, and somebody else had replaced them, it almost wouldn't make any difference. There are a lot of answers to that question, but basically, no, we don't regret it.

DM: Is Seaside still an experiment for you?

EPZ: I think it is an experiment until it is done. Actually, it will be an experiment for many years, because the life of the town will evolve. We will see what happens, if we are lucky enough to see it built out, which would be a rare achievement. If you look at the work of John Nolen or Eliel Saarinen or any of the other people who have done town planning, and you see how many times the effort has been stymied or interrupted along the way for various reasons, the fact that Seaside has been built to 50 percent or more is quite remarkable.

DM: In the interview three years ago, Andres wasn't optimistic at all that Seaside could be completed in the way it was intended. What do you think today?

EPZ: I think there is a really good chance of it because, in fact, most of the remaining lots have been purchased, and they will be built out within several years as their predecessors have been. It will be very interesting to watch it in ten years, in twenty years; in fact, I think that there are certain assurances that it will continue to be a pretty great place, judging by the planned communities that have retained their controls over the years and that already exist in the United States. I am thinking of places like Coral Gables or Santa Barbara.

DM: You talked a moment ago about all the different people who have designed at Seaside, and the fact that even if that mix had changed in some way, it wouldn't have mattered that much. But I want to point out to you that almost all of those people come from a younger generation of practicing professionals; in some cases, it is their first real built work. Was this intentional on your part when you declined to design everything at Seaside; in fact to encourage many other younger people to work there?

EPZ: I think the answer to that is no. The code was written assuming that for second homes in that part of the country, most people would never go to architects; the houses were either going to come out of magazines or be done on the kitchen table or by plan services, judging by what we were seeing in that area. So the code was really written, to some degree, tongue-in-cheek. That's not exactly true, but we were looking at houses that had six different window types, which made us think that window proportions should be coded; we assumed the worst common denominator would reign. So many good designers have gotten involved with it that, in a way, it is not a true test for the code, or the architectural guidelines. Still it has been a fascinating experiment because it has been stretched in other directions that we didn't anticipate. We realized after the first couple of commissions that Seaside was providing an opportunity for young designers, part of a phenomenon that was occurring in this country in the 1980s in which developers and the financial world began to see that design was important to production and sales. Robert Davis has always been

18.
Appell House
Architect: Victoria Casasco
19.
Chatham House
Architect: Walter Chatham
20.
Hybrid Building
Architect: Steven Holl
21.
Krier/Wolff House
Architect: Leon Krier
(Photos: David Mohney)

18   *19*

an enthusiast of good design, so the participation of young designers was encouraged for several reasons.

DM: How has Seaside been received by the academic side of the architectural profession?

EPZ: Variously . . .

DM: Let me put it another way: what kind of criticism have you had, what intelligent comments have you received about Seaside, and where have they come from?

EPZ: Some of the criticism has been that the controls are too stifling. That comes from both academic and legal quarters, or just lay people who believe that in America there is a tradition of no control, which is not true. Too much control is one criticism that has been levied, that we can argue. (We are of course capable of arguing all the criticisms.) Another one was that the code produced too much of a style. Architects especially were responding (at first) to the Victorian, then to more postmodern, imagery, and then to the outright classicism of some buildings. But the fact that all three exist, plus the new stuff like Victoria Casasco's and Walter Chatham's houses, proves that the codes are not merely stylistic. Most of the criticism is that it is too something or other, or that it is too homogeneous, in terms of everything being new and bourgeois; but of course, how could it be anything but that in its first generation?

DM: Do you find that the criticism changes, when critics who think they understand Seaside, but haven't visited it, come and see it?

EPZ: That happens a lot. But there are people like Deborah Berke who haven't come to terms with themselves for designing in a vernacular mode for southerners in a resort, when their work is supposed to be offer-

ing some sort of polemic to northeastern architects. She has done some wonderful buildings there, and I think her current work, the manufactured housing (which she is a little too reticent about), is really wonderful, and she should be capitalizing on it more.

That's part of a bigger picture in the world of architecture with respect to art, and whether architecture and urban design are art. Are art and design accessible to the general public? I think that many designers and artists are taught in school that their work should not be immediately accessible to the general public, because that would not be sophisticated enough. And certainly the work and proposals of people like Peter Eisenman support that. Even Frank Gehry's work, which is never explained, yet can be analyzed according to rational criteria, is presented in a mysterious high-art fashion, which I think is not necessary.

DM: Do you think that is one of the problems with the public perception of the Steve Holl building?

EPZ: Well it might be perceived as a part of that syndrome, but . . . I don't think the Holl building was trying to make itself inaccessible. Most of the local criticism of the Holl building is a reaction to the fact that it is the first four-story town center building, and seems out of scale without the others around it to complete the square. Also, it faces a blank party wall to the highway, while the front lot awaits its own building.

But accessibility is the crux of the discussion these days. It's not style and it's not postmodernism, or classicism, but I think it comes down to, and certainly every architect or artist or designer has to deal with, relating to an audience. In the twentieth century, most of us have chosen to relate to a specialized audience, rather than take on multiple audiences. Sometimes that discourse

20

21

on multiple levels takes place in the public media, magazines, and newspapers, but I don't think it does in architectural criticism. It does in politics or literature or science, but not in architectural criticism.

DM: Do you find that there is a bias in academic culture in America against suburban design and its consideration; that in fact it is thought to be sub-urban and thus less worthy of attention than what are traditionally considered to be urban design issues?

EPZ: I think there is that, certainly, in the world of architecture. However, there is a tremendous interest currently—academically—in the study of suburbs in other disciplines. And despite the still overriding preoccupation with object buildings in architectural design curricula, there are more and more academic programs seeking to design in the suburbs specifically, such as ours [the University of Miami], Stefanos Polyzoides at USC, Doug Kelbaugh and Peter Calthorpe at the University of Washington, Bill Morrish and Catherine Brown at Minnesota, and Max Underwood at Arizona State. I don't think any of us feel this is an avant-garde issue, but we do agree that the suburbs are the precursor of the twenty-first century city, and if architects are not going to provide the vision for the new city, who will?

Ironically, and this goes back to your question about the academic criticism, there has been very interesting academic and professional support from geographers and historians, who are observers of the urban scene. They see something like Seaside or the town-planning movement, which is beginning to occur as a very inter-esting initiative to control things that have just evolved. Planners and landscape architects are more defensive about it, because it is an indictment of what they have

been doing for the last forty years. But certainly there are a lot of people, especially people involved in growth management, which is a varied group of people, in terms of training and discipline, and broad ranging in their concerns (planners who are involved in growth management are, by its demands, broad ranging in terms of disciplines; they are not merely specialized), who think it is very exciting that somebody is putting all these concerns they have verbalized into physical form. Planners and politicians and elected people have had a terrific response to it. The other support has come from ecologists, who see in the approach to existing conditions, in the willingness to deal with native landscape and regional, ecological issues—as well as the implications that town design has on the reduction of automobile use and pollution—they see this as really supporting what they have been saying about the planet.

DM: What do you think of Leon Krier's house, which is his first built work?

EPZ: I think it is wonderful. It was exquisitely built. It has a great character; it is a house which is of a very specific character, that I don't think will be matched except by exact copy. I know a lot about it, so that certainly is not a first impression. I've seen it evolve with life-size details that were drawn and then sent to the carpenters, and then discussed and revised on site in a real working relationship. And I've also seen the designer laugh at himself for first of all designing a house, which he has always said should be part of vernacular fabric and not architects' work, and second of all for putting a temple on a house, which is the second rule of his own that he broke.

I heard that a week ago or so, Leon and Rita came

from the airport to Seaside, to see the finished house for the first time. A lot of people were there to watch them see the house. Rita was about to enter the house when Leon called out, "Stop!" and he picked her up and carried her in.

DM: That's a wonderful story!

EPZ: It certainly takes its place among the loveable buildings of character, which, if they were not as good as they are, would be dangerous or sore thumbs in their positions. Certainly each of us has a catalogue of this kind of building, connected with experiences we cherish.

DM: I think it is an exceptional house as well, but I have to say that I was a little surprised by its study. It is the room at the top of the house that is almost hidden by the temple that you spoke of; to me it had a sense of a ship's bridge. It is clearly a room for one person; but that's not a problem as much as the connotation of its view down across the whole town; that in fact this was the captain in charge of the ship that is Seaside.

EPZ: It is a bit of a folly, yes . . . and that is an interesting interpretation, and a valid one; Seaside is some kind of offspring of the first theories that he espoused about European cities. So that is one perspective to take on it which is amusing, but I don't think it gives the whole picture, because it doesn't give enough credit to the multiple influences in Seaside, both from history and current theories, and most of them are American.

DM: Have people confused Leon's influence on the urban design?

EPZ: With . . .

DM: Yours.

EPZ: Sometimes. I think there have even been some articles in Britain which say that he is the designer of Seaside, but I take that as just misinformation.

DM: I would suppose that that is less true now than say three or four years ago, when Seaside was first emerging into public discussion.

EPZ: It hasn't happened too much. And there have been articles that have come out with Robert Davis as the designer, as well. But considering how much media description of the place that there has been, I think the facts are pretty straight. Likewise, I think that Robert could think that a lot of the architectural publications haven't given him credit, so I'm sure there are inequities that people have felt, but I don't think any of them are overwhelming. Although there is one building that has remained inappropriately anonymous, which is the first beach pavilion, designed by Ernesto Buch; it has appeared all over the place.

DM: It is the icon of Seaside.

EPZ: Without his name on it, which is a shame, because he is an excellent designer and his ability is growing, too.

DM: I spoke a couple of weeks ago with him about this, and he had a very nice attitude about it, that it had been subsumed into the public culture as the emblem of what Seaside is; he was just very happy about that, and it didn't matter who had done it, but the fact that it had such a strong iconography meant that it simply took care of itself.

EPZ: That's nice to hear. It is being used in all sorts of imagery related to other parts of Florida in the local media. We found a Palm Beach magazine for tourists that had it on the cover.

DM: It has been in television commercials for Florida in the New York area.

22

22.
Tupelo Street Beach Pavilion
Architect: Ernesto Buch
(Photo: Steven Brooke)

EPZ: Eastern Airlines was using it in a poster, and they never even flew anywhere near Seaside! (Laughter)

DM: Two of the downtown buildings are finished. In the context of initial urban design, what do you think of them, and do they provide a critical mass of the idea of the town in your eyes at this point in time?

EPZ: No. I think actually that it is a very awkward point in not having more than those two, in particular because one is two stories and one is four stories, and it really leaves the people who don't know hanging about what the next thing will be. If there is not more downtown building, it is really going to feel incomplete, so we are really hoping that more of that can happen quickly.

DM: What about the first question, in the context of your initial ideas about the downtown area; do they fit with your preconceptions about it?

EPZ: I don't think that we were anticipating either of these two, but they are certainly doing the right things in terms of the codes and the mixture of uses they have in them, and I think that their scale will be justified when there are more of them. Right now people are having trouble with their scale.

DM: You said earlier that it is a matter of their isolation to some point, and once there are others among them that will be mitigated to a great extent.

EPZ: The question always was, within the configuration of that downtown, where to start. Starting in the center would have taken care of the rest of it never being built out, but that would have been too distant from the road: right now the new buildings have at least a tenuous connection to the other commercial area—the restaurant across the street. But it is at an awkward point, and the question now is, do you continue to grow circularly around the octagon, or do you balance it by doing something on the other side? A designer would probably prefer the balance, but real life retail issues will probably push the continuing development from one side around toward the other.

DM: Can you pick a favorite building at Seaside, and a least favorite? I'm putting you on the spot a little . . .

EPZ: I couldn't give a favorite building, because I think that there are so many neat ones; I think I told you when we were there together that every time I go there I want to rush down the street and into every new house to check it out; they are almost like toys.

DM: That's a good point to turn to this question: your personal experiment at Seaside of turning away work, of refusing to design any of the buildings yourselves in the interest of encouraging original variety in the hands of many different designers, seems somewhat paradoxically to have rewarded you. You have a stellar reputation among your peers, and a plethora of projects on your desks. In other words, by turning away a relatively small amount of work some years ago, I think that it has brought you much more work. Is that a fair assessment, and does this situation offer any lessons to other designers?

EPZ: I don't think that it is that directly connected. The amount of work we have comes from the fact that Seaside has been building out with such great care and such success, which of course does have a lot to do with the fact that so many people have been involved with it. Everybody involved with it was lucky that it was a good idea at a good time. Robert could have decided not to go ahead with it, he could have sold it to someone, any number of things could have happened. There is a touch of inevitability to it, because it

23.
Aerial view of Seaside, 1989
(Photo: Michael Moran)

23

successfully weathered an economic recession in that area. So the one thing that normally would stop building (over which architects don't have any control) did not. I think that, among other things, gives it a tremendous credibility and poignancy.

In general, however, giving stuff away tends to be positive in the long run. We both believe that, and while we weren't thinking in those terms in the beginning at Seaside, we have certainly realized along the way that it is a very productive way to work. The communication it forces among architects, and the fact that now we always work with several other architects or other firms in most of our town plans, is only rewarding for everybody, and the plans can only be better by that much consensus work tending towards a single goal.

From what I understand, this is a very different kind of situation for the profession than some years ago, when there seemed to be a much more territorial aspect about work. Nevertheless, it is very important to realize that collaboration is successful in urban design, in which many different actors can be builders and designers, rather than in single buildings. Buildings need strong concepts and should be of strong character of a unified nature. Urban design profits from focused and single-minded goals as well, but there is room for many expressions. It is enriched, in fact, by multiple expressions.

DM: What do you think the future of urban development in America will be?

EPZ: I can talk about what I would like it to be, which may be different than where it is heading. In terms of architects working in cities, I think that unfortunately there is a large number of designers who are still, or once again, working in a specialized, individualistic, and fragmented manner of one building at a time. They contend only with the limitations of that commission, or that program, or that artistic moment, as we have been doing for many years now. But I think it would be really interesting and productive, a whole new era, if we could manage some sort of national overview of our cities, which would recognize the enormous waste in our downtowns and urban areas that have been abandoned and discarded in many cities in the last forty years, in order to lay waste to the land outside of those cities. I think it is an unprecedented exchange of inefficiencies.

Since we have been learning a little bit more about the kinds of controls that occur in other countries, where the resources of both city fabric and rural or natural environment are much more carefully husbanded, it seems more and more ridiculous that we should keep going this way. So the growth management movement, if it were to continue (and of course the whole building sector of the economy is highly suspicious of it, and in many places is mounting strong enough attacks that I think its future is not certain), and its relative, the historic preservation movement, could lead to a very interesting new era in, with new attitudes towards, our cities. In fact, there is a public groundswell, both in the preservation movement and in the ecological movement, which supports many architects' ideas about cities. It is happening as a grass-roots movement of people who want to save their towns, or people who understand that urban growth cannot keep sprawling outside cities, and that it is time to rethink building, to go back to the existing infrastructure of center cities, and to restructure the suburbs.

The Germans have a method (as an American, I hesitate to describe something that seems to go against all our inalienable rights of property ownership): the municipality decides when a town needs to expand. When that occurs, the agricultural land at the edges of the town is condemned, and purchased by the municipality at agricultural prices. The city plans it, puts in the infrastructure, and resells it for development, and the profits go into paying for that infrastructure. It doesn't mean that better design occurs, as you can tell around the periphery of European cities, but at least it takes growth and development out of the realm of land speculation and individual greed, and the political process is not the determining factor for what is good for the land or the city, as it is in the U.S.

DM: How do you see your own position in this possible future?

EPZ: We have tried to be conscious of how we can be most effective, and we have made it our goal to get as many good projects built as possible, trying to hit as many of the big generic issues as possible: for example, towns that are attached to malls—what do you do with the malls, how do you retrofit existing shopping centers to become town centers, and what happens to downtown redevelopment. We are very conscious of trying to do case studies that have a good chance of being built, because we have seen how effective Seaside is as a built project. What you said about people going there and being convinced is so true; we've seen what a difference that makes. So we're convinced that it is very important to provide the example that people can refer to, as possible successes, or to help point the way. We think that teaching is a very important aspect of it, too. Also, getting the word out correctly is important; we

have a great fear of something that is already happening, that some people think Seaside is just a style, that it is not an urban or spatial concept, that it is just the surfaces of the buildings. A lot of the established planning firms that are referring to Seaside in their presentations have not really learned what the spatial concepts are, and just think that this is the next thing to do, that it sounds great, that they can just go zooming in and it is going to happen. They don't realize there is an enormous amount of design training that produced the planning principles of Seaside. It was really quite thorough academic research on the part of a number of people involved in it that made the forms that are there work. We are always running into people who think, "Oh, yeah . . . this is exactly the right thing, and deals with so many different issues which are so important, and we really want to do it with you," and you get involved with designers who, because they do not have the design training or experience, just cannot make it happen. There is a rigor of design there, in doing it right, which is really important. This is not an age in which that is valued, even by many architects, because personal expression still takes the upper hand over empirical information.

DM: That is a very good, but general, answer. Can you be at all more specific in terms of your own position?

EPZ: (Laughs) Like should we be running the Department of the Interior, or something?

DM: Well, at its most extreme, is this a burgeoning crusade? Are you and Andres crusaders? I would consider you among the leaders in this movement. Are you comfortable with that assessment, and do you see yourselves being able to continue it for a substantial period of time?

EPZ: I think we see it as a mission. It has become that by the multi-disciplinary support we have encountered, which made us realize that to some degree there is a responsibility here. And we realized that because of Seaside and a number of other things that have occurred since then, such as the twenty-plus towns or urban projects we have worked on in the last couple of years. Right now we are at the forefront of people designing this sort of thing, just by dint of academic background and practical experience. We know about building and "the market," all of the development issues, and now growth management issues as well. We have design experience, and credibility with clients, because of this broad-ranging background. But hopefully there will be people along with us very shortly if they are not there already. There are people like Dan Solomon and Peter Calthorpe, Steve Petersen and Barbara Littenberg, Rodolfo Machado and Jorge Silvetti, and lots of other people, who just haven't had the opportunities we have had to prove themselves, so to speak, to the people (the developers or the cities that hire them) who make these things happen. So I think that we are not going to be out front very long, not alone very long. But that's still a general answer, isn't it?

DM: I think it is specific enough. It is probably dangerous to get any more specific than that.

EPZ: I think we should write something about what we know. We should impart a list of rules, of whatever. It is on the agenda.

DM: Two last questions: in a conversation with Neil Levine at Seaside last summer, he pointed out that he thinks Seaside is unique because there has been an equality between men and women in the project from the beginning and in all facets of the work. That is something that is quite unique in the urban design and architectural world. Do you think that is true?

EPZ: I think you have trouble as soon as you try to say there is equality, because someone is bound to say, no, there isn't yet, but I think that he is probably right in observing there has probably been much more input by women than in any other urban project.

DM: Then let me put the question a different way: are women on equal footing with men at Seaside, and have they been through the whole course of the project?

EPZ: That is a difficult question to answer. Women are not yet on an equal footing with men in architecture anywhere, not just at Seaside. But here they are probably in as good a position as they have ever been in a building and architecture project such as this, or of any sort (except for people like Julia Morgan). Yet I'm sure that Deborah Berke or Melanie Taylor or Victoria Casasco would give you an earful about problematic situations. And Daryl, Robert's wife, is an unsung hero. She has been an enormous contributor to the aesthetic of Seaside; she has a really good eye. A lot of the details that make the place—that many people (buyers) responded to—and her whole aesthetic in running the marketplace have made an enormous contribution to the life of the town, in an unquantifiable way.

Some of us [women] measure ourselves and our work against an ideal objective standard, shrinking from its impossibility, setting up impediments to our own growth in a way that men don't. There is always the bigger issue—and I don't think you can get into it here—of opportunities not taken up readily by women in practice because they are not recognized as such. I mean that we don't have the background to ask

24.
View from the Tupelo Street gazebo looking west, with the Seaside water tower in the distance (Photo: David Mohney)

24

straightforwardly for certain things when we could. However, I think Neil is correct in saying that there probably have been few building projects of any scale in recorded history where women have been as prominent as here. I think it has a lot to do with the time in which Seaside was spawned. It was a time in which men were freeing themselves of old patterns, too; certainly for Robert Davis to set out on this project in the manner in which he did is a sign of the times. He wanted to make a place rather than a monument, or a place that could be monumental; I think that is a very important part of it.

DM: Is modernism over?

EPZ: I don't think so. I think it is alive and kicking.

DM: And you are trying to kick back?

EPZ: I would wish that one-dimensional modernism were over. I think there is still terrific ground to be covered by both modernism and tradition, or pre-modernism, I might say, together as part of a history, of a continuing history. I mean, modernism is already a tradition. We have experimented with pre-modernism in all sorts of ways as a centered, holistic, focused design effort, as well as the more fragmented approaches taken recently, and I think that it would be worthwhile if modernism could experiment with a non-object-oriented type of design.

You might think of something like town design in terms of modernism, and they are not necessarily anti-thetical. Certainly early modernism with its ideology was very conscious of providing housing and places for people to live and work, and lead integrated lives. That was one of the ideologies of modernism, actually making design and art accessible. The fact that it resulted in the opposite is a supreme irony. So, it would seem

that there is still a great deal of ground to be covered in the evolution of that initial ideology, which then does not separate it from pre-modernism as much as it might seem to have been. So I am actually very excited about things like the Steve Holl building and the houses that attempt to be modern within the context of a community, or a larger whole. I think it has appropriate social ramifications.

At the university, we were talking about all the different ethnic groups that are there now, and how they all have their support groups, and whether that is divisive or unifying in the end. What I suspect about cities is similar to what people are hoping for in the multi-ethnic situation of the university, or in this country now, or even in the world. One of the things we are learning from designing communities is that if each neighborhood (and you can even take this down to each building in a town) has a strong identity of its own, perhaps there can be a clearer communication across these differences than when you don't recognize any differences at all. Maybe that is a little bit of what has been happening at Seaside. In spite of the fact that many houses have been clamoring for attention, there is still a common basis for communication for them all in the street. One would hope that for a city, its center is the one place that all the people from its different neighborhoods can come together, whatever their character or income level or ethnic group. Public space provides that opportunity, and that is one good reason that we should stop neglecting it!

The interview with Andres Duany took place at Seaside in the summer of 1986. The interview with Elizabeth Plater-Zyberk was conducted over the telephone in the fall of 1989.

Andres Duany and Elizabeth Plater-Zyberk

A Town Plan for Seaside

Andres Duany and Elizabeth Plater-Zyberk have become leaders of a new generation of architects and designers who claim a significant role for design in contemporary planning and development issues. Trained as architects, they have focused their efforts in urban design and town planning forcing a reconsideration of the design arts in the day-to-day planning process. The urban and architectural codes for Seaside are presented in a simple, graphic manner (pp. 98–103) and balance the need for a visible form of shared urban organization with the opportunity for individual architectural creativity, to achieve what they call the "authentic variety" of valid urban experience.

Duany and Plater-Zyberk consider Seaside to be an on-going experiment. As successive phases of the building plan are achieved, they are able to evaluate the results and make any necessary adjustments to the plan and its code. Early in their work on the project, Duany and Plater-Zyberk decided that in order for the experiment to be judged fairly, they should not participate in the building program. Consequently, from the beginning of the project, there was no single design point of view imposed, or even implied. As a result, a large number of people—some trained professionally, others acting as interested amateurs—have designed buildings at Seaside. The code was written with a clear understanding that people of diverse architectural backgrounds would be working within the town.

Much of the pair's talents as urban designers derives from their ability to understand the workings of towns, both in a physical sense (understanding the relationships of setbacks to street widths, for example) and in an administrative sense. Their most recent efforts have been concerned with writing the urban codes for new towns, which often determine their physical form. Their practice combines investigations of prototype and theory with analysis and invention. They have applied the results of this research to a number of built projects. Seaside also introduced another feature that has become standard in their practice: the design charrette. This is a four- to ten-day event that brings together all of the professionals needed to produce an urban design: engineers, consultants, planners, administrators, local officials, designers, and the public. The charrette has the advantage of dramatically reducing the time needed to create an urban design. Furthermore, the direct interaction intensifies and improves communication amongst the collaborators; the result is, more often than not, a unified scheme.

Based in Miami, Duany and Plater-Zyberk's practice has received national and international attention. The architects have received prominent awards from both public and private organizations, as well as state and national chapters of the American Institute of Architects. Both lecture extensively, and have taught at major architectural schools throughout America. They were instrumental in establishing a new program of suburban studies—the first of its kind—at the University of Miami.

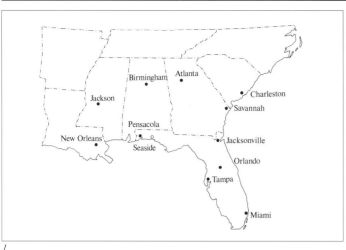

1

1.
Regional map
Note the relative proximity of such cities as New Orleans, Birmingham, and Atlanta, as compared to Miami

2.
Aerial photograph showing the beginning conditions of the town, 1979

2

3.
*Plan by Robert Altman prior to
Arquitectonica taking up the commission. The central rectangle marks the
first phase.*

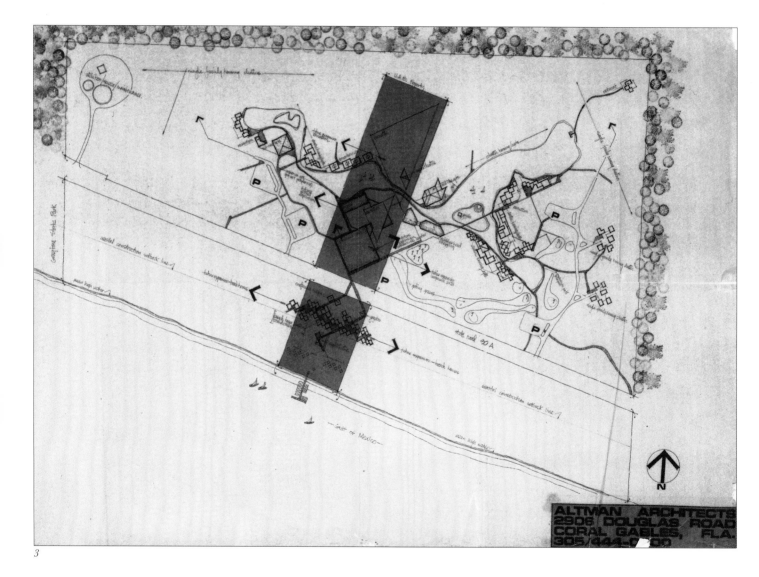

First design by Arquitectonica (Andres
Duany and Elizabeth Plater-Zyberk,
partners in charge) showing a four
block "downtown" intersection, inland
"cabins" along a curved path, and
"cabanas" at the shore organized as
an exhedra. The water tower

terminates the axis inland and the
beach pavilion terminates it seaward.
Certain ideas were retained in the
final plan: the urban core, the pavilion
at the end of the street, and the
differentiation of dwelling type by
location rather than program.

5–7.
Details

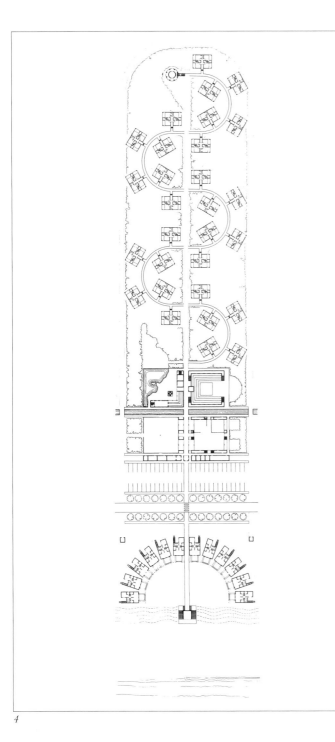

4

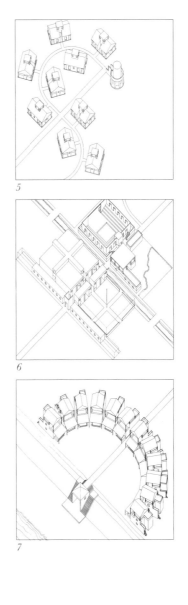

5

6

7

12.
Leon Krier's redrawing of the plan showing many refinements. Among these are the narrow greenbelt and the mid-block pedestrian alleys (known as "Krierwalks" in the Seaside vernacular). The plan manifests a general willingness to distort the geometry of the private parcels in favor of a more perfect definition of public space. This attitude was generally implemented, but not to the extent proposed by Krier, because it was thought to be too complex for a new town in America.

13.
Leon Krier's rendered version

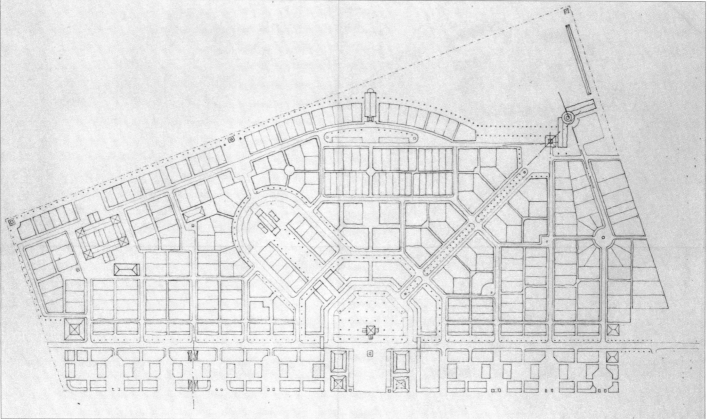

12

13

14.
*The "final plan" as rendered in water-
color for marketing purposes. The plan
is being built with minor modifications.*

15.
*The first sketch showing modifications
made in response to Krier's comments.*

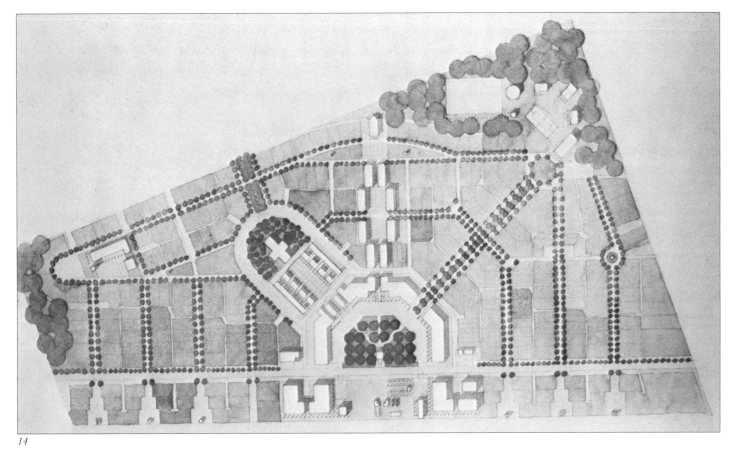

14

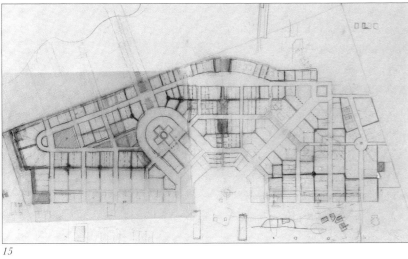

15

16–18.
The street sections as drawn at the charrette. These were an integral part of the design of the building types.

19.
Studies for Type I buildings executed at the charrette and later. The code was based on these studies.

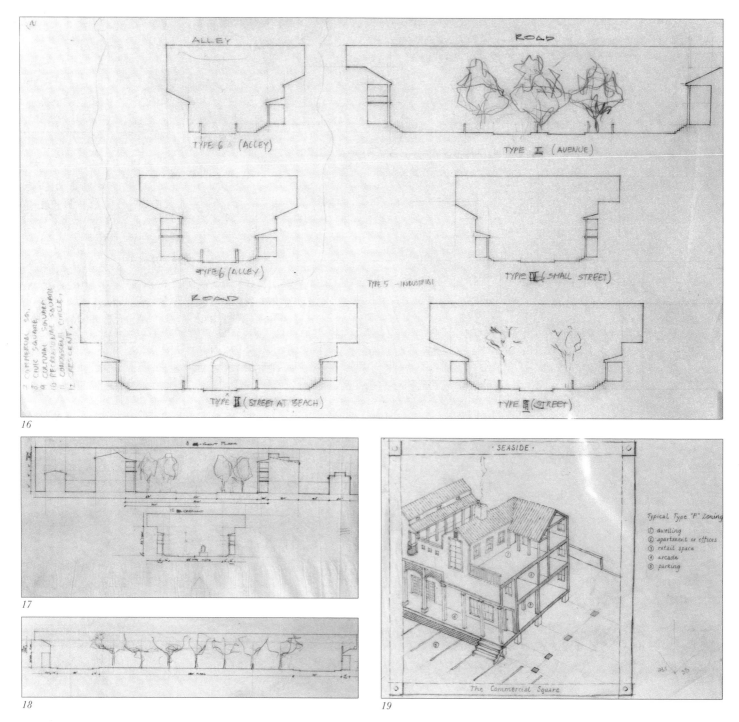

16

17

18

19

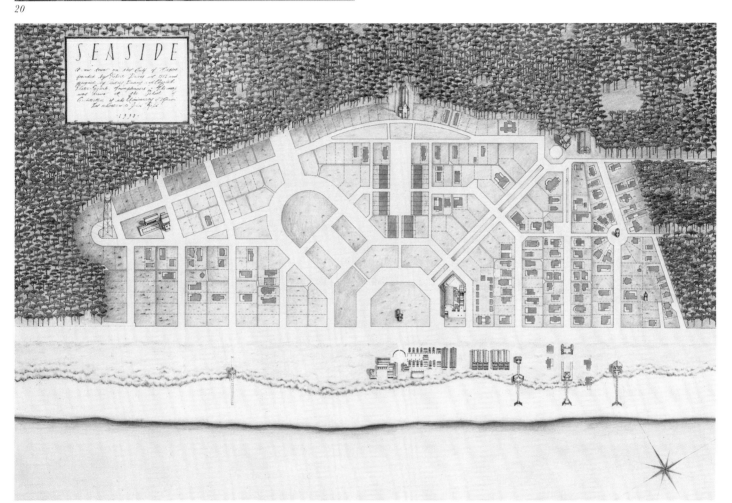

20

20.
The urban code was used in a full scale test at Catholic University in 1983. Under Professors Dhiru Thadani, Gregory Oaksen, and Peter Hetzel, 140 first- and second-year students designed and built models of every building at Seaside. This experiment was executed in the absence of anyone associated with Seaside.

21.
Colored-pencil rendering, 1990; prepared by Miami University students, supervised by François Le Jeune.

21

*The final draft of the urban code
drawn at the charrette. The format of
this code was invented at this time.
The notion of specifying building type
as a way of achieving spatial definition of public space was considered
relatively un-American, but it was
thought to be necessary in the absence
of an urban tradition in the contemporary American design profession.*

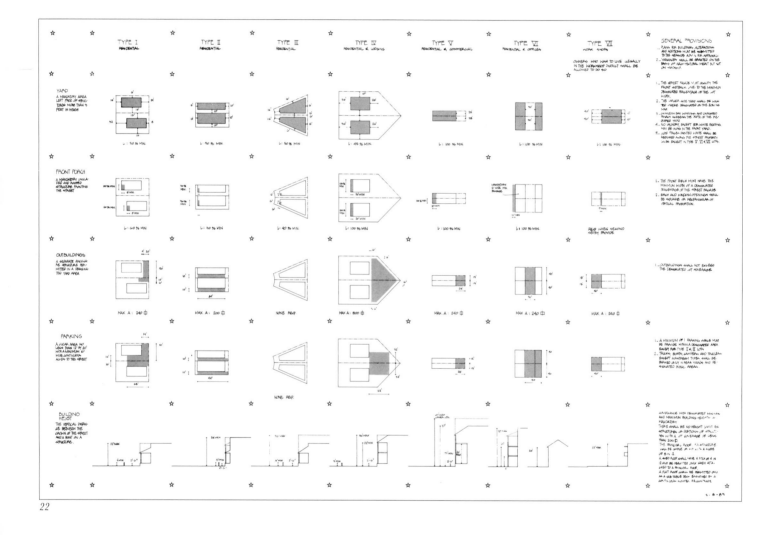

23.
The current urban code (CAD version). This document incorporates the results of extensive testing with students at the University of Miami. This document is easily fine-tuned as designers find small ways to subvert it.

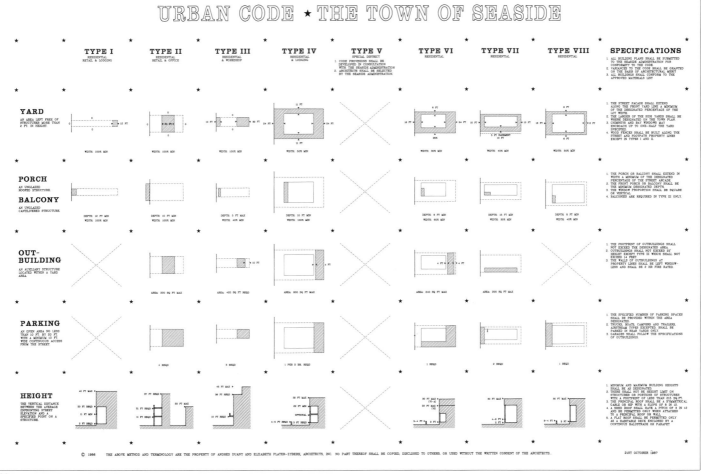

URBAN CODE ★ THE TOWN OF SEASIDE

23

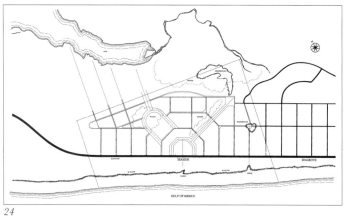

24

EXISTING CONDITIONS

The layout of Seaside responds to pre-existing and man-made conditions as follows. Two large gorges providing access to the beach determine the location of the central square and the easternmost street. Existing wooded areas are preserved along the diagonal avenue and in open areas around the tennis club and city hall. High ground determines the location of the tennis club and one of the small squares. A central square opens to the south, increasing the building frontage on the ocean. The existing grid of Seagrove Beach to the east is received and extended to provide multiple access points and social continuity. The new street grid is left open to the north allowing access to the inland lake at some future time.

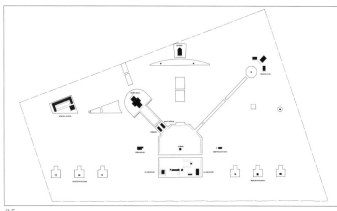

25

PUBLIC BUILDINGS

The major public buildings (town hall, school, chapel, and tennis club) are located inland to activate those areas farthest from the shore. These buildings are bound to the central square by corresponding public spaces: secondary square, major avenue, and market square. Pavilions at the termini of each north-south street belong to the residents of these streets. Two larger clubhouses in the central square provide beachfront colonies for residents of the east-west streets. The southern portion of the central square will contain small public buildings responding in an ad hoc manner to changing needs in the early years of the town. The plans of the public buildings as shown in the drawing are hypothetical, since most have not yet been designed, or are only now under consideration. Public buildings are not subject to the urban code except for the provision that they be painted white, which is to insure public identity despite a size that could often be less than that of private buildings.

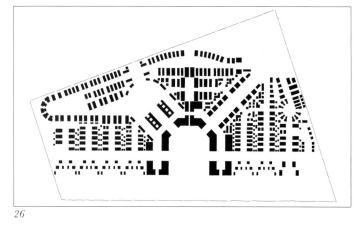

26

PRIVATE BUILDINGS

The private buildings may be houses, apartments, shops, offices, hotels, motels, or workshops. Building forms will be generated by the provisions of the code as interpreted by many designers. Building uses are not strictly controlled as in conventional codes, but loosely determined by a conjunction of specified building form and urban location. This drawing approximates how Seaside would be completed if the building envelopes were all filled to the maximum.

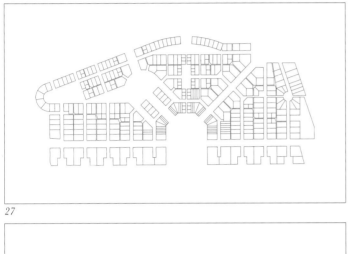

27

PRIVATE LAND

The proportion and dimension of lots are specifically related to their intended use and building type. In order to provide a relatively neutral urban fabric and to facilitate marketing, most lots are standardized, but others do not avoid the idiosyncratic characteristics that generate unusual buildings to serve as landmarks. There is a gradual downsizing of residential lots towards the center of town in order to increase density.

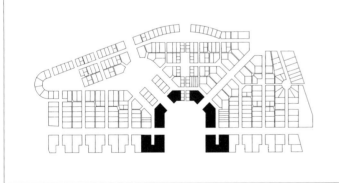

28

TYPE I

These lots define the large central square which straddles Route 30–A with a decisive spatial act. Type I zoning is intended for retail uses on the ground floors with residential above. It will probably generate hotels and rooming houses, especially on shoreline lots. These are the tallest buildings at Seaside, with a maximum of five stories permitted. They are party-wall buildings with no setback at the front, where a large arcade is required. A great deal of variation is permitted in the heights. The prototype for this type is found in main streets throughout the South, although seldom in so continuous a manner.

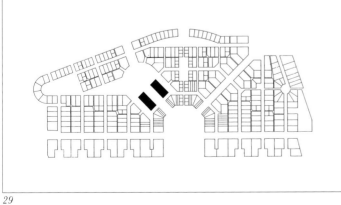

29

TYPE II

These lots define a small pedestrian square at the front of the town hall. Type II zoning is intended primarily for office use although apartments and retail establishments may occur. The code generates four-story buildings with courtyards and smaller buildings at the rear. The provision affecting arcades and silhouettes is highly specific and only minimal variety is possible. It is intended that this square will have a decidedly more sedate and dignified appearance than the central square. The prototype is found in the Vieux Carré district of New Orleans.

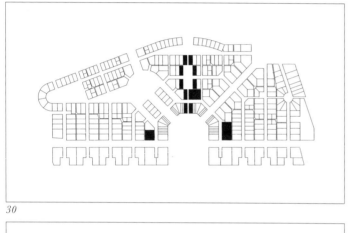

30

TYPE III

This type generates two uses ultimately determined by lot size and location. Large lots face the service street at the rear of the central square buildings. Warehouses will occupy these, probably for storage, workshops, and automobile repair. A fire house and service station will also be located in this zone at lots abutting Route 30–A. Smaller lots occur along the north-south pedestrian route that connects the church with the central square. These should generate small shops, and it is hoped that a Sunday market will be housed on these premises. Type III generates party-wall buildings with few restrictions other than a limit on height.

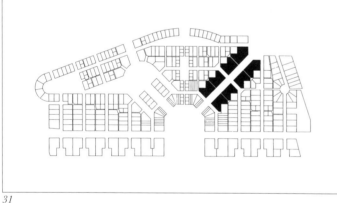

31

TYPE IV

These are large lots that line the avenue connecting the central square to the tennis club. Type IV zoning generates large freestanding buildings with substantial outbuildings at the rear. This type may become private houses, small apartment buildings, or bed-and-breakfast inns. The setbacks on all sides, together with a continuous porch mandated for the street front, should result in buildings of some grandeur. The prototype is the Greek revival mansion of the antebellum South.

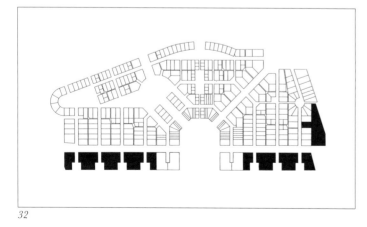

32

TYPE V

This type is a special category for large lots that can contain several buildings. The Seaside code, like other codes that depend on the street front as the baseline for prescription, is too rigid in its control of site plans several lots deep. Consequently, there is a minimum of prescriptions and it is required that the lots be planned as coherent groupings, with the provision that the designs be approved by the municipal authority.

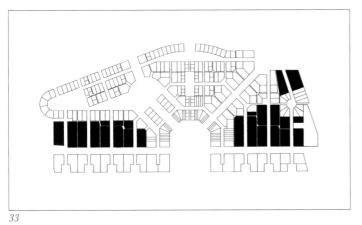

33

TYPE VI

These lots are the suburban section of Seaside. They occur on north-south streets where there is a view of the sea at the end of the street corridor. Lots become slightly smaller toward the center of town for a gradual increase in density. Type VI zoning generates freestanding houses and encourages small outbuildings at the rear, to become guest houses and rental units. The requirements for substantial front yards secure the sea view for inland units. Picket fences help to maintain the spatial section of the street, which would otherwise be excessive. The prototype is found everywhere in the suburban and rural South.

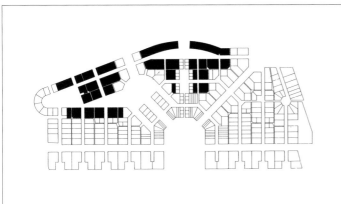

34

TYPE VII

This type occurs along the east-west streets where no view of the sea is possible. The lots are, therefore, smaller and less expensive. Since a view corridor is unnecessary, the front setbacks are minimal. A zero setback is permitted along one of the sideyards so that houses tend to generate private yards to one side. The Charleston "single house" is the prototype.

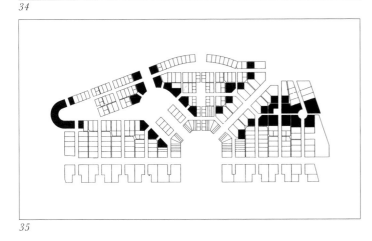

35

TYPE VIII

This type is more liberal than others in its prescriptions. It is dispersed throughout the residential areas of the town. It occurs at locations that require some degree of acknowledgement as gateways or special places.

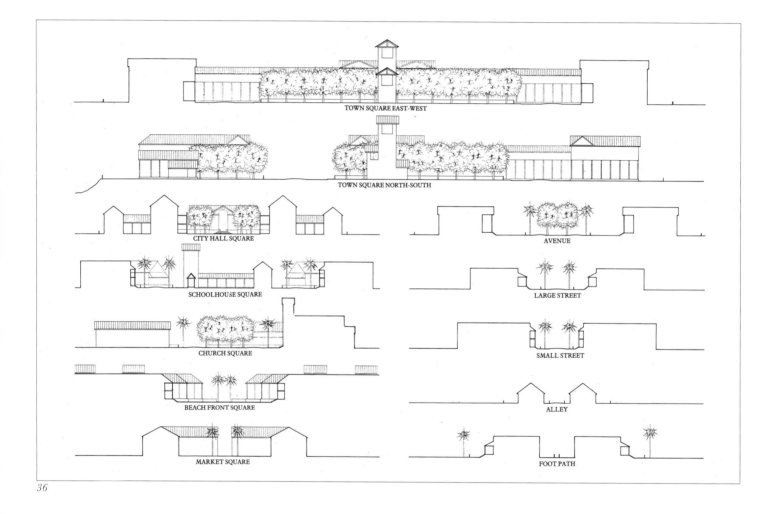

TOWN SQUARE EAST-WEST

TOWN SQUARE NORTH-SOUTH

CITY HALL SQUARE

AVENUE

SCHOOLHOUSE SQUARE

LARGE STREET

CHURCH SQUARE

SMALL STREET

BEACH FRONT SQUARE

ALLEY

MARKET SQUARE

FOOT PATH

37.
Seaside, 1988
(Photo: Michael Moran)

37

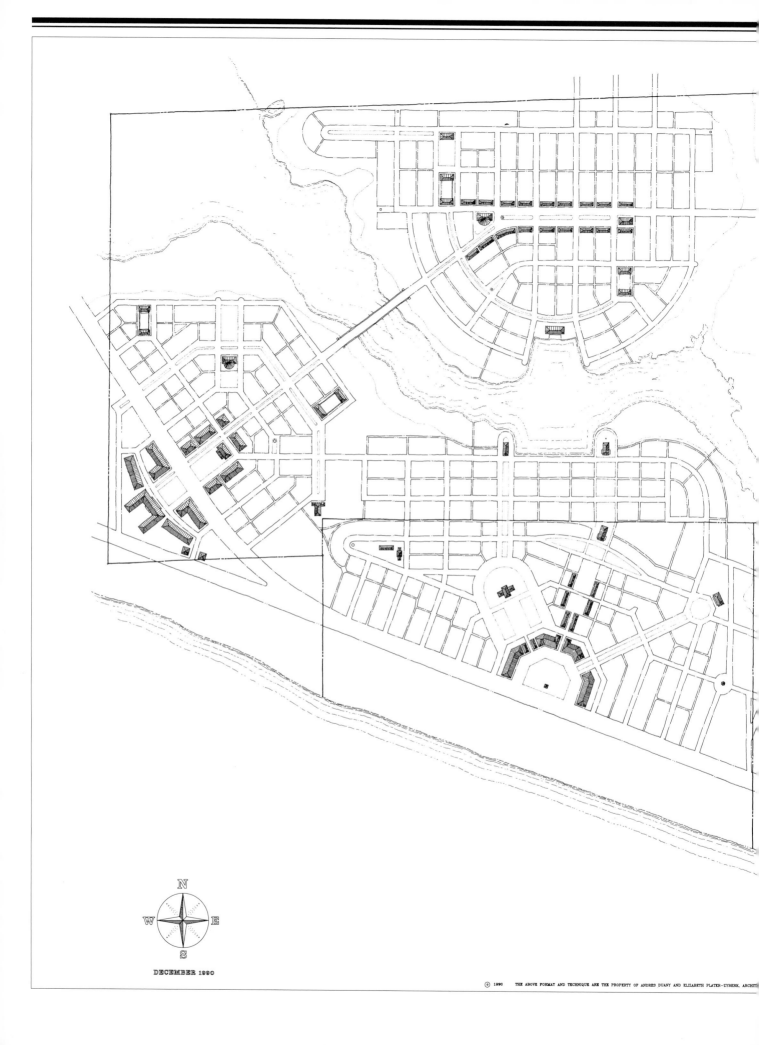

DECEMBER 1990

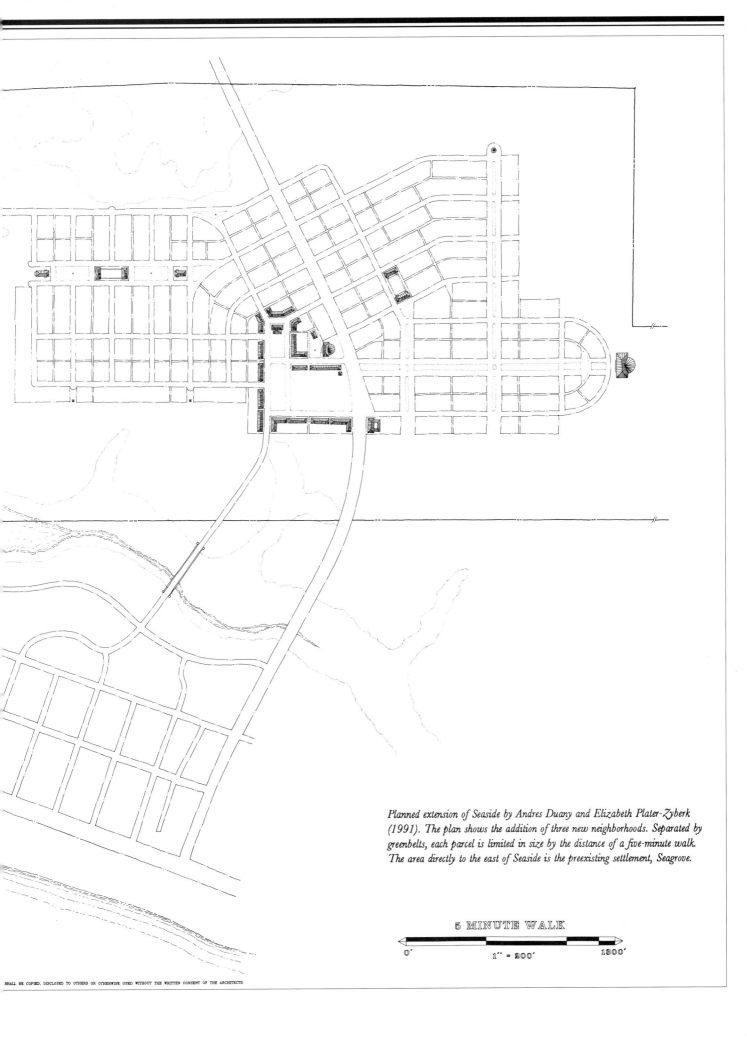

Planned extension of Seaside by Andres Duany and Elizabeth Plater-Zyberk
(1991). The plan shows the addition of three new neighborhoods. Separated by
greenbelts, each parcel is limited in size by the distance of a five-minute walk.
The area directly to the east of Seaside is the preexisting settlement, Seagrove.

5 MINUTE WALK

0´   1´´ = 200´   1300´

Robert Davis

After receiving a degree from Harvard Business School and before beginning work on Seaside, Robert Davis worked with a conventional real-estate development firm in south Florida. His efforts at Seaside, however, have run counter to many typical development rules. First, Seaside has been developed slowly, with only half the town built during its first ten years. This has allowed an ongoing evaluation of the town to affect subsequent work, whether in code revisions, style, or adjustment to an existing building in order to adapt to the changing circumstances around it (e.g. Market District, p. 114).

Second, from the beach pavilion to the garden architecture in Rosewalk, the public realm has had a clear physical manifestation. While the cul-de-sac on the golf course was a familiar arrangement of conventional developments in the early 1980s, Davis took a vastly different course, investing instead on buildings and street fixtures that help to establish a public domain and transform a development into a town. Third, he has lived at Seaside since work began on the town, and his daily participation in the events there has encouraged quality in the building process.

Robert Davis is a throwback to an earlier age, when educated people were expected to be conversant of architecture, among many other arts, and, for the most part, he has taught himself about the history, theory, and beauty of architecture. In 1990, the American Academy in Rome awarded Robert Davis the prestigious Rome Prize in Architecture.

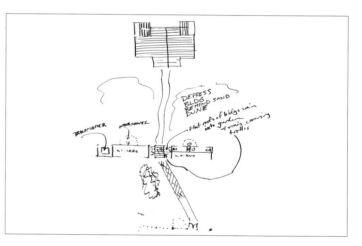

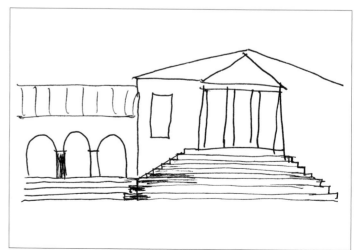

Davis House

Davis House
Robert Davis with John Seaborn
1.
Oblique view from the rear
2.
View from Seaside Avenue
(Photos: Michael Moran)
3.
Rear elevation
4.
First floor plan

1

2

3

4

Dogtrot House

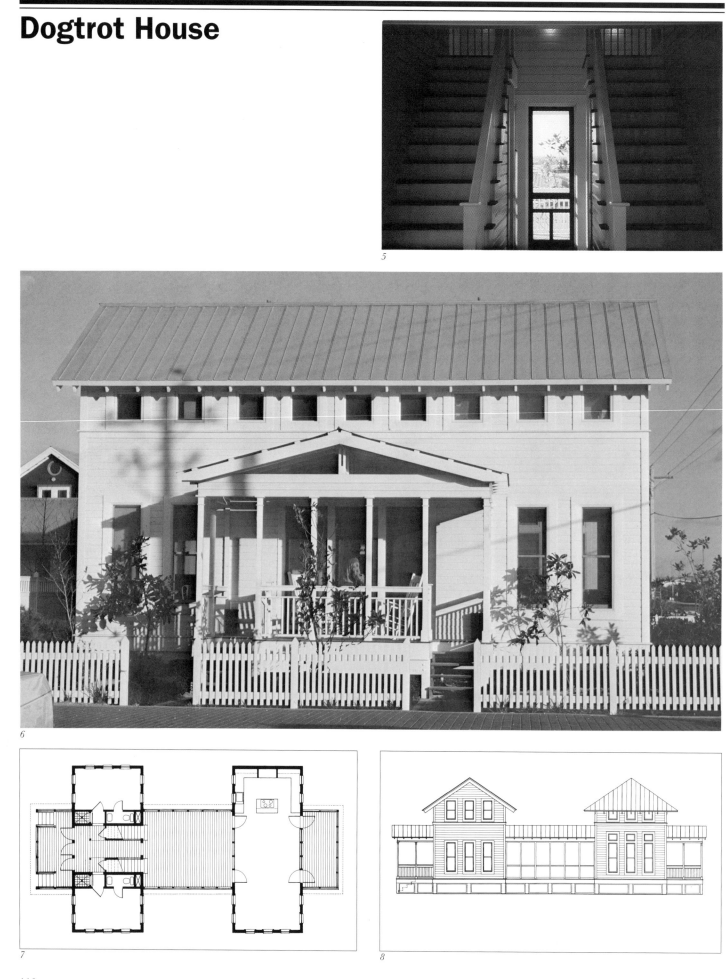

5

6

7

8

Post Office

9

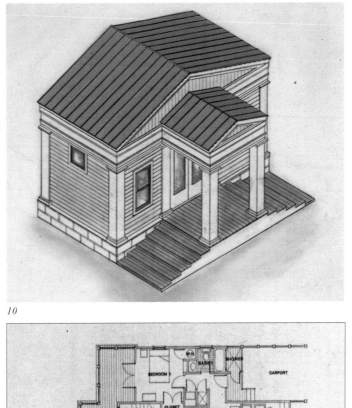

10

11

Ernesto Buch

Tupelo Street Beach Pavilion

Ernesto Buch was a member of the original team that participated in the Seaside urban design charrette. He has designed two public structures for the town, which are both widely admired. The Tupelo Street Beach Pavilion, on a prominent location (adjacent to the state highway, and near the edge of the town) was the first pavilion to be built. It did much to define an image for the town, as well as to establish a high standard for construction at Seaside. A subsequent generation of architects and builders were inspired by the simplicity of its classically-derived plan and elevation, and by its elegant wood construction. The Public Works Building is notable for its polychrome exterior and unrefined building materials (tree trunks as columns, for example). It is a dressed-up vernacular building with a utilitarian plan.

1

Public Works Building

1.
View from beach
(Photo: Steven Brooke)

2.
View from Forest Street
(Photo: Steven Brooke)

3.
First floor plan

4.
Second floor plan

5.
East elevation

2

3

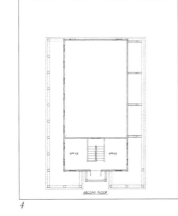

4

5

Various Architects

Market District

1.
Plans, 1981–85
2.
Bird's–eye view, 1989
(Photo: Deborah Berke)

Over a period of five years, early in the construction of Seaside, a group of buildings was added to, transformed, and rearranged on a yearly basis by a variety of designers. This flexible approach to accretional urban growth has been a model for the development of the town as a whole. These structures in the market district have served as offices, shops, restaurants, porches, terraces, and dune walk-overs. In the early and mid-1980s, they defined Seaside's downtown area, since all residential building was confined at the eastern edge of the town.

1

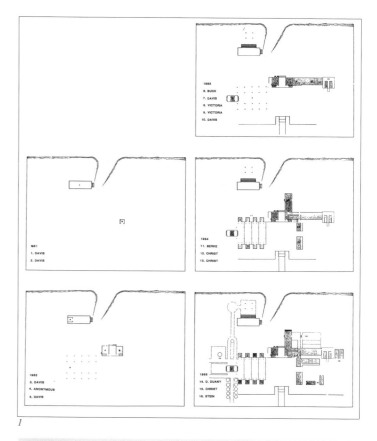

2

Teofilo Victoria

Market Pavilion

1.
Central pavilion
(Photo: Steven Brooke)
2.
Axial view
(Photo: David Mohney)

Teofilo Victoria originally worked on Seaside with Arquitectonica and then returned to work on the first master plan with Andres Duany and Elizabeth Plater-Zyberk Architects. He was the first Town Architect; and at the time his office and apartment was an actual sharecropper's cabin trucked in and installed next to the only other structure, which was nicknamed the "shrimp shack." Victoria renovated and "dressed up" the shrimp shack to create the central pavilion of the open-air market. (Deborah Berke was largely responsible for the overall design of the market as an agora-like arrangement of pavilions.)

For Victoria the design process was a hybrid of two different means of analysis: rationalist analysis with European origins and typological analysis of Southern vernacular types. Both methods derive their ideas from construction and lead to a particular understanding of style and building type in Seaside.

1

2

Joanna Lombard

Beach Club and Guest Cottages

Joanna Lombard is an architect who practices and teaches in Miami. The beach club was an early project in Seaside's history, planned before the urban design was complete in all its details. It was intended as a Type V complex—a gathering place and social activity center for the residents of Tupelo Street—however, with revisions to the urban plan, the site of the beach club was made available for residential use, and the project was not executed. The Tupelo Street beach pavilion, built some time later, assumed some of the functions originally intended for the beach club. Lombard's sketches indicate an attempt to use vernacular architecture within a rigorously formal site strategy.

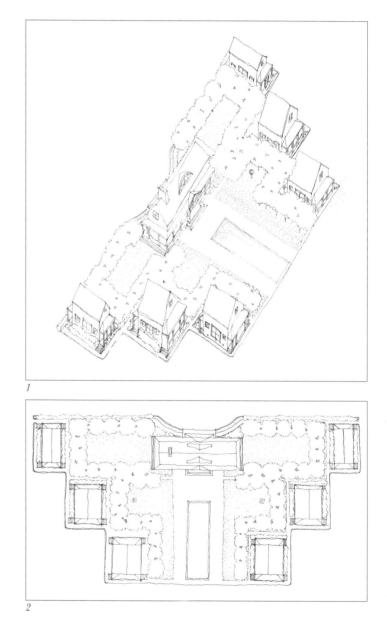

1

2

1.
Axonometric
2.
Roof plan
3.
First floor plan, alternative scheme

4.
Composite drawing: roof and tower plans, and elevations
5.
Composite drawing: plan and elevation, alternative scheme

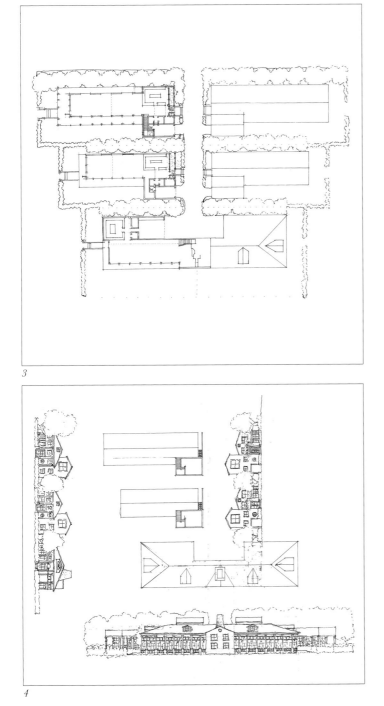

3

5

4

Deborah Berke

Hodges House

Deborah Berke lived in Seaside for the better part of a year, from 1982–1983, and has continued to design buildings at Seaside on a regular basis since that time, while maintaining her own practice first in Washington, D.C., then in New York City. Despite this seemingly continual involvement with clients for Seaside, Berke regards herself as a member of the "loyal opposition" to the Seaside codes, especially to the "stylistic homogeneity" which developed in the early stages of the town's history.

Berke has had the opportunity to work in a variety of Seaside's house types, and several of her projects have served as models for other builders and designers. Her Averett Tower project was Seaside's first tower, and did much to define that genre. Her designs are characterized by crisp plan arrangements and elevations. Berke's interests in architecture extend from town planning to modular housing prototypes for the late twentieth-century American home. She teaches at the Yale School of Architecture, and is presently in partnership with Carey McWhorter.

1.
View from street
(Photo: Steven Brooke)

2.
Site plan
3.
First floor plan
4.
Second floor plan

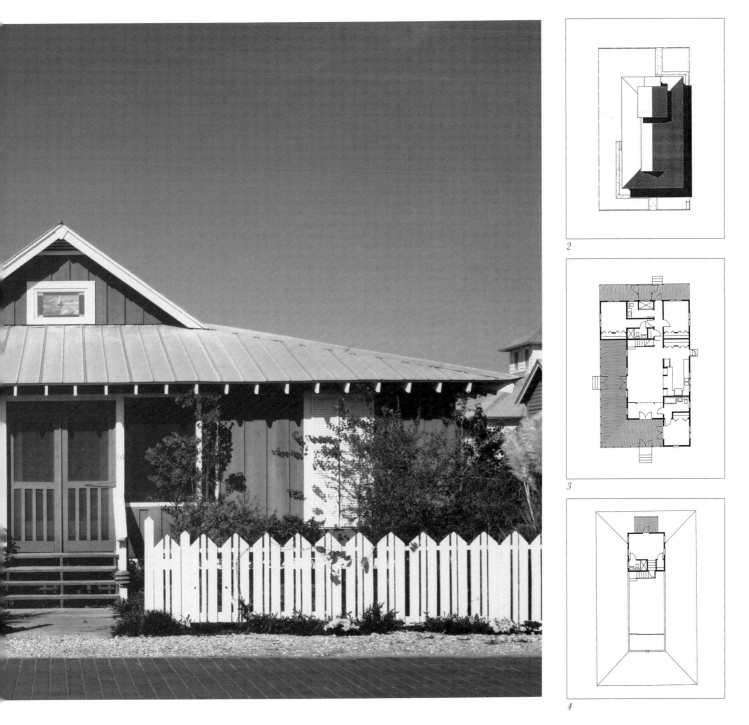

2

3

4

Averett Tower

5.
First floor plan
6.
Second floor plan
7.
Attic plan

8.
View from path
(Photo: Steven Brooke)

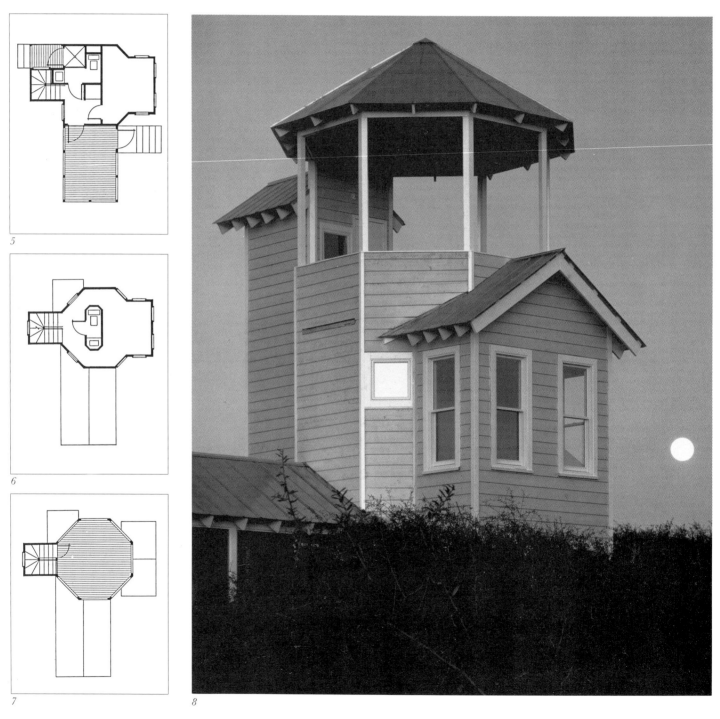

5

6

7

8

Gray House

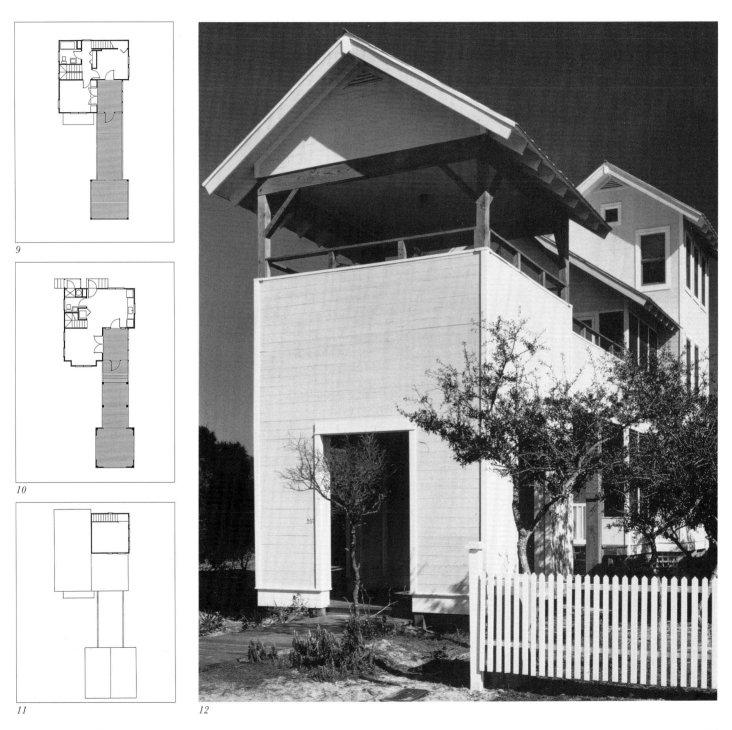

9

10

11

12

Wright House

13

14

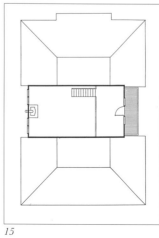

15

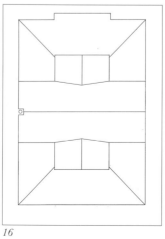

16

Sward House

17.
View from street
(Photo: Steven Brooke)

18.
First floor plan
19.
Second floor plan
20.
Roof plan

17

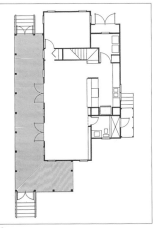

18

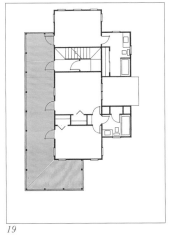

19

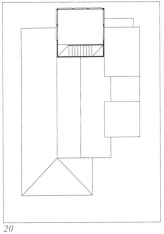

20

Gray House II

21.
View from street
(Photo: Steven Brooke)

22.
First floor plan
23.
Second floor plan
24.
Roof plan

21

22

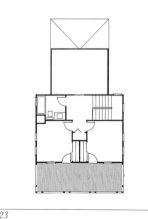

23

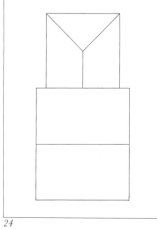

24

Childs House

25.
View from street
(Photo: Steven Brooke)

26.
Site plan
27.
First floor plan
28.
Second floor plan

25

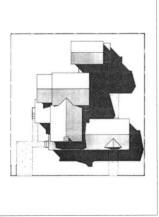

26

27

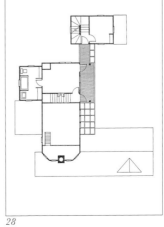

28

Brinkman House

29.
View from street
(Photo: Steven Brooke)

30.
First floor plan
31.
Second floor plan
32.
Roof plan

29

30

31

32

126

Averett House

33

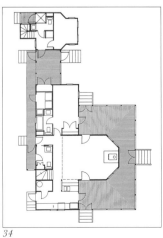

34

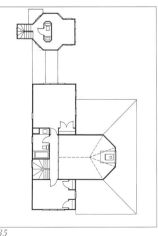

35

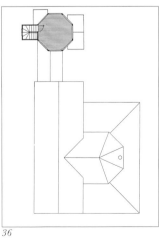

36

Sward House II

37.
View from street
(Photo: Carey McWhorter)

38.
First floor plan
39.
Second floor plan
40.
Roof plan

37

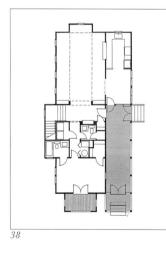

38

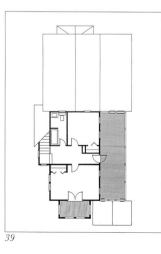

39

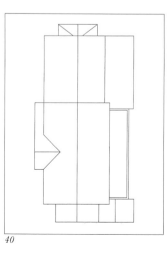

40

Jones Compound

41.
View from street
(Photo: Steven Brooke)

42.
First floor plan
43.
Second floor plan
44.
Roof plan

41

42

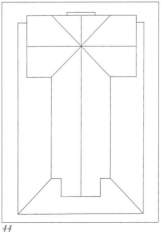

43

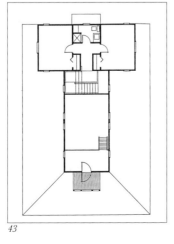

44

Gray House III

45

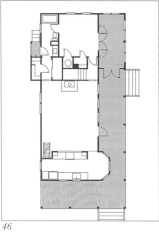

46

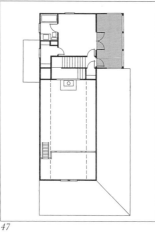

47

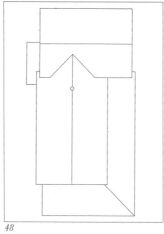

48

Berke and McWhorter

Schmidt House

49

50

51

52

Modica Market

53.
View from central square
(Photo: David Mohney)
54.
Section

53

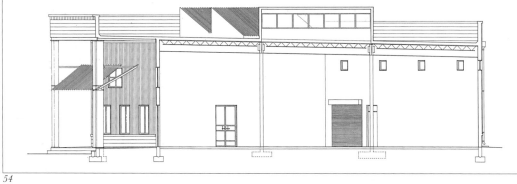

54

55.
First floor plan
56.
Perspective

57.
Detail
(Photo: Steven Brooke)

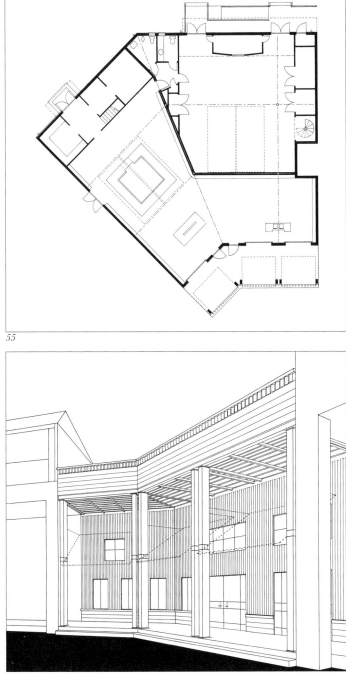

55

56

57

Carey McWhorter

Hudson House

Although this is the only project for which McWhorter takes sole credit, his involvement with Seaside is lengthy. While he was a graduate student of architecture, he served as a summer intern at Seaside, and assisted with some construction. As an associate of Deborah Berke, he was largely involved in the design and documentation of several of her projects. This project is intended as a prototypical house in the fabric of the street. As the architect describes it, "The house offers . . . a sincerity of images rendering an almost style-less, unselfconscious participation in the town as a whole . . . . This attitude towards style serves as so much beachside 'grey flannel,' fitting this dwelling in the social uniformity of the leisure class." McWhorter is currently in partnership with Deborah Berke.

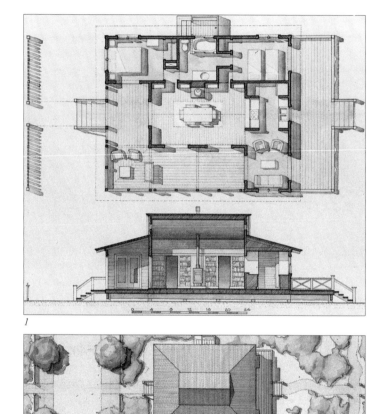

1

2

1.
Plan and section
2.
Site plan
3.
Perspective

3

Caroline Constant and Cameron Roberts

Fire Station

The fire station was one of the first in a series of public buildings designed for Seaside. The architects displayed an interest in utilitarian prototypes, which were often studied by the first designers working at Seaside. In the evolution of the fire station design, two types emerged: the simple shed and the civic building. A utilitarian shed housing two fire trucks faces the alley and a low masonry building containing an office, sleeping quarters, and storage space extends along the main highway shielding the proposed warehouses from public view. The fire station was to serve as a town meeting hall and a work building until other public buildings were completed. Public buildings are not subject to the provisions of the code; thus, the fire station was not required to have wood construction—its primary materials are concrete block and corrugated metal siding.

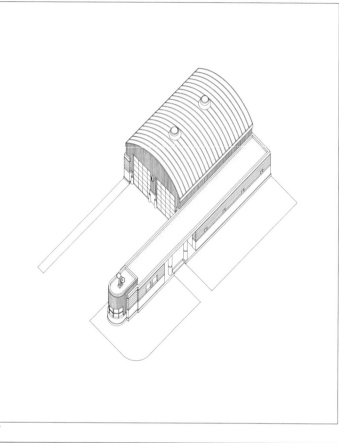

1

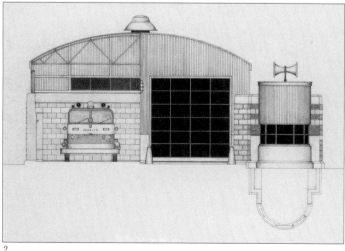

2

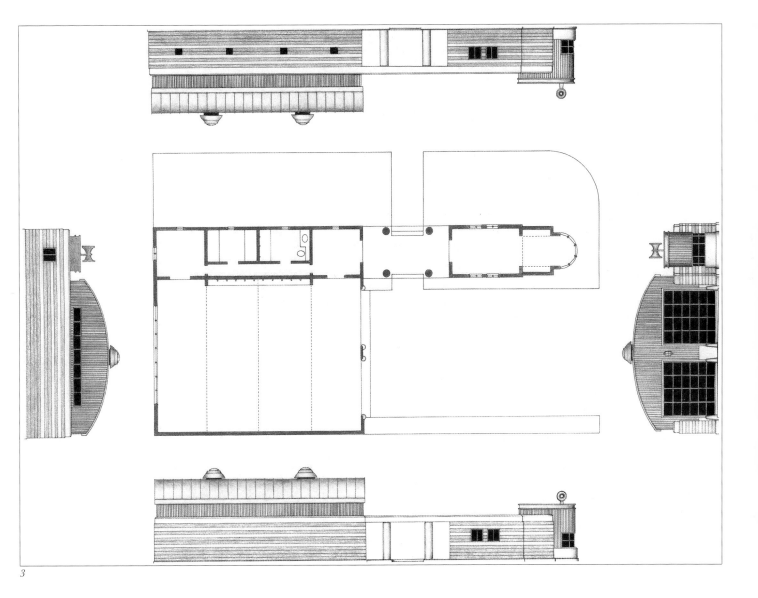

3

Robert Orr and Melanie Taylor

Rosewalk District

Robert Orr and Melanie Taylor were among the first architects to work at Seaside. At the time, only Tupelo Street had been developed. They were asked to design a scheme for an oddly configured site at the edge of the town, just east of Tupelo Street, which had been designated Type V. Orr and Taylor chose to develop the site for fourteen houses and a common garden. In their practice they had long valued buildings conceived in terms of the public spaces that they occupy. They attempted to make a kind of miniature urban grouping to preview the character of the town as a whole. In an effort to preserve existing vegetation, the houses and other garden structures were arranged picturesquely within the site. The houses at Rosewalk were some of the first two-story structures to be built at Seaside. In the ensuing period of Seaside's growth, a number of houses in other parts of the town imitated the Rosewalk cottages in color, proportion, and detailing.

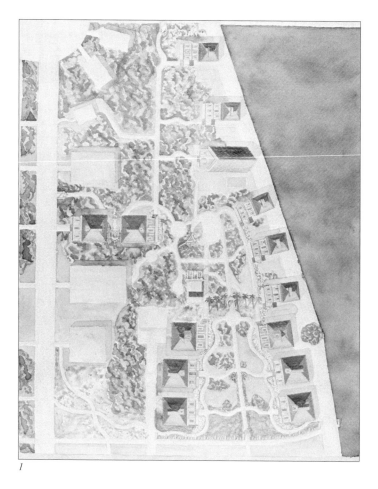

1

1.
Site plan
2.
View of Rosewalk (from left to right)
Dreamsicle, Veranda Classic,
Town House, Breezy Bungalow
(Photo: Steven Brooke)

Breezy Bungalow
3.
Side view of porch
(Photo: Steven Brooke)
4.
First floor plan
5.
Second floor plan

2

3

4

5

Rosewalk District

6.
View through rose trellis
(Photo: Orr and Taylor)

Veranda Classic
7.
View from garden
(Photo: Orr and Taylor)
8.
First floor plan
9.
Second floor plan

6

7

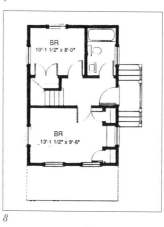

8

9

140

10

11

12

10.
Queen Anne's Cottage perspective sketch
11.
Chess pavilion
(Photo: David Mohney)
12.
Garden furniture
(Photo: Orr and Taylor)

141

Robert Lamar

Winslett House

Robert Lamar has been involved with Seaside in a variety of capacities since the early days of the town's history. He worked with Robert Davis in the preparation of several of the early town structures, most notably the post office and the Tupelo Street gazebo. He assisted Orr and Taylor with the construction documents for the Rosewalk houses, and Derrick Smith in the preliminary design for the University Inn. His own work at Seaside consists of several houses and a variety of unbuilt projects.

1

2

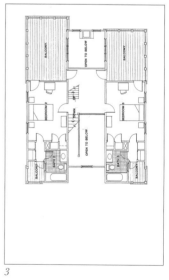

3

University Inn
Schudde House

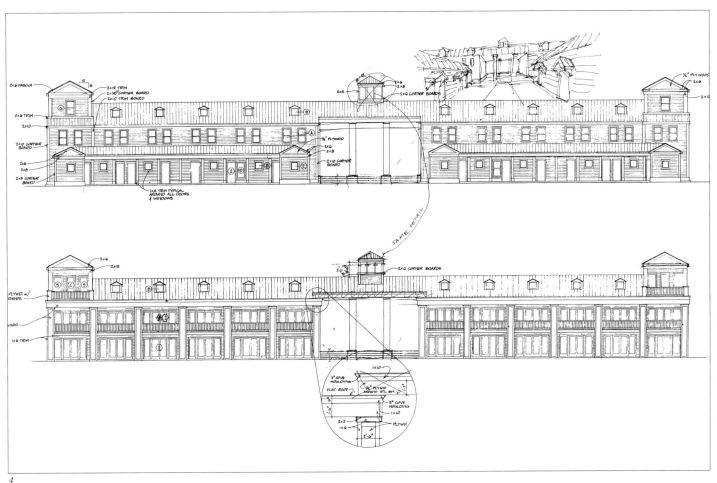

4

5

6

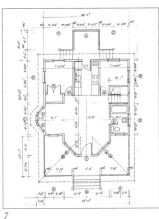

7

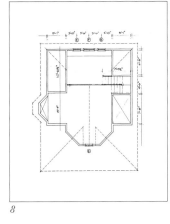

8

143

Derrick Smith

Beach Pavilion

1.
Perspective sketch
2.
Elevation
3.
Plan

While a student at the University of Miami, Derrick Smith became one of the first Town Architects. The challenge of Smith's early residential projects was to transform vernacular building types with contemporary plan requirements, while preserving their informality as well as the ineffable qualities associated with wood construction.

Inspired by the architecture of nearby small towns and guided by the rigors of "American Vignola," Smith rigorously attended to his own hybrid of classicism and American vernacular. The beach and pool pavilions were important early experiments concerning the urban space of the street. Similarly, in the houses, the space of the porch is regarded as an element belonging both to the house and to the street.

1

2

3

Pool Pavilion

4.
*View from corner of Savannah
and Forest Streets
(Photo: Steven Brooke)*

4

Miller House

5

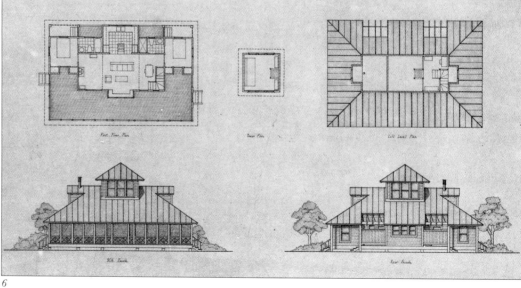

6

Stein House

7

8

University Inn

9

10

11

Patrick Pinnell and Heather Cass

Church

For Patrick Pinnell and Heather Cass the public buildings and institutions of Seaside offered an opportunity to deepen the experience and character of the town beyond that of a vacation spot. Architecturally, the institutional buildings—by maintaining simplicity in form and construction—potentially contain a critique of some of the more particular detailing in individual houses. The design is a type of pantheon with one face towards Seaside to the south and another face to the cemetery on the north. The geometriesof the scheme were chosen for their cosmic or numerological significance; for example, a half round of a twenty-four-sided polygon was given twelve faces for the twelve months of the year and for the twelve apostles. In general, the scheme was meant to create form that was emblematic of ritualistic assemblies, drawing from archetypal sources like the Greek amphitheatre. The building was intended to be used by a number of different denominations, as well as to provide a place for town meetings and social gatherings.

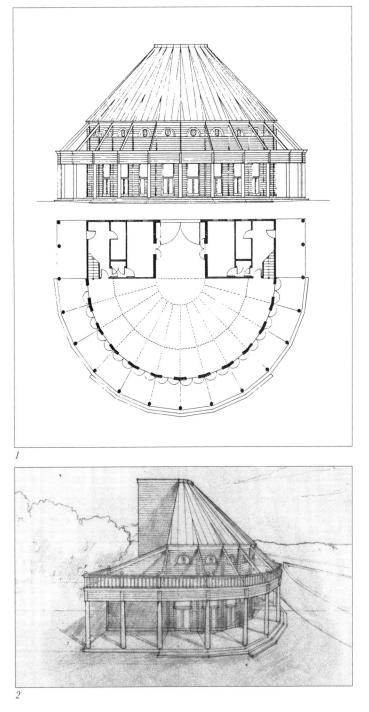

1

2

Advance Design Planning Service

Doyle House

Much of Duany and Plater-Zyberk's early thinking about the urban code was intended to accommodate projects executed by a plan service. Before land values escalated, it was anticipated that many Seaside houses would be designed in this manner. This is a traditionally accepted practice of designing houses in America, and should Seaside serve as a model for resurgent small town urbanism, it could have widespread application. The Doyles dealt with Advance Design Planning Service directly. The entire project is presented on one sheet of drawings.

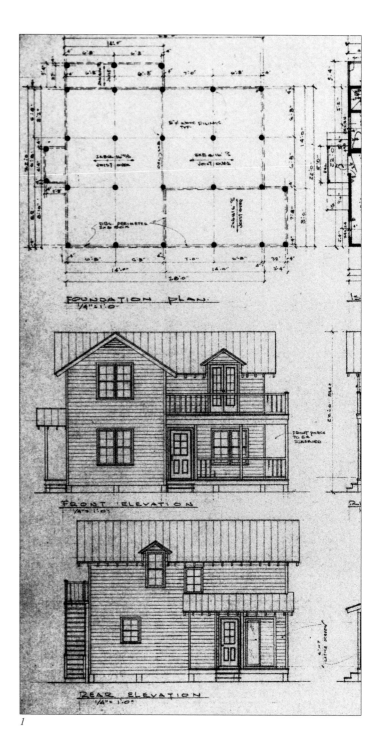

1

1.
Construction drawing: (clockwise from upper left) plans, site plan, wall section, and elevations

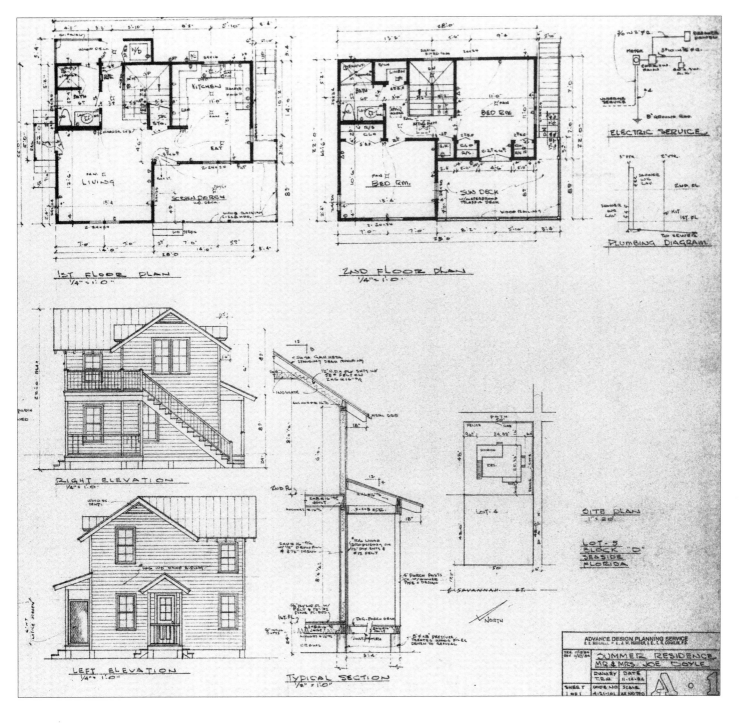

Tom Christ

Savannah Street Beach Pavilion

Tom Christ, an architect based near Seaside, has built more structures in the town than any other designer. His work encompasses almost all the residential types set forth in the urban code, and is distributed widely across the town. (A recent amendment to the urban code now limits designers to no more than a dozen residential projects at Seaside.) In his houses, Christ typically links together a variety of masses, with the porch always a prominent feature.

The Savannah Street Beach Pavilion was the second pavilion to be built. As a series of simple elements, spread out but linked together, the structure makes an interesting contrast to the Tupelo Street Beach Pavilion which preceded it. The long, ramped series of steps that cross the dune down to the beach also set a precedent for later pavilions.

1

1.
View from beach
(Photo: Steven Brooke)
2.
Front elevation, early scheme
3.
Side elevation, early scheme

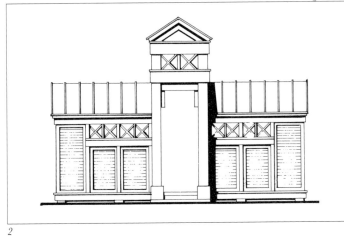

2

3

Hudson
House

4.
Front elevation
5.
Side elevation
6.
First floor plan

Tucker
House

7.
Front elevation
8.
Side elevation
9.
Side elevation

4

5

6

7

8

9

Bruno House

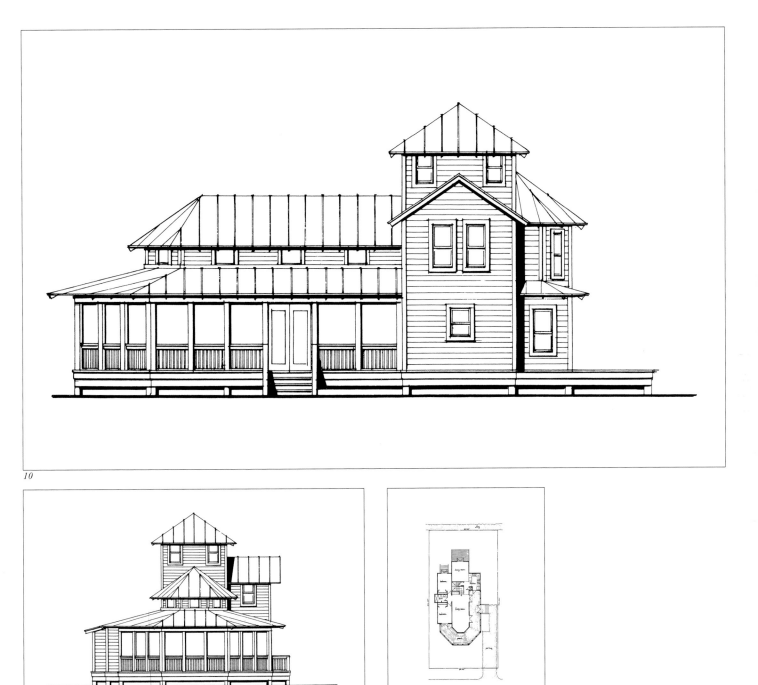

10

11

12

155

Robert A. M. Stern

Seaside Hotel

The Seaside Hotel was an early project that helped to develop a vision of the town's public areas. The main wing contains the lobby and public functions of the hotel, most of which are raised to take advantage of the views of the coastline. Generous verandas under broad overhanging roofs are in keeping with the character of Seaside's residential architecture. A bridge spans the state highway (Route 30–A) connecting the main wing, which runs parallel to the beach, to a secondary wing that defines the town square. The secondary wing houses retail space behind the covered arcade and the hotel rooms on the floors above. Rooms are strung along open-air, single-loaded corridors, affording views of the ocean and access to porches. Stained wood siding, metal roofs, and wood balconies capture the informal quality of many of the local buildings. Ultimately, the hotel program was limited to the beachfront site, while the secondary wing was built out by Steven Holl as the Hybrid Building.

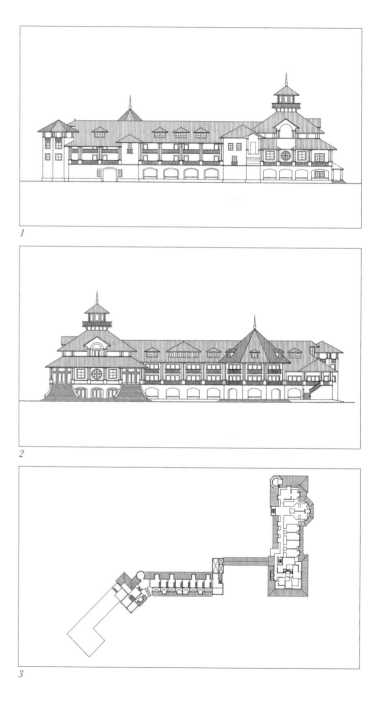

1

2

3

1.
North elevation
2.
South elevation
3.
Fourth floor plan

4.
Model, beachfront elevation
(Photo: Robert A. M. Stern Architects)
5.
West elevation

4

5

Stuart Cohen and Anders Nereim

Seaside Condominiums

With each new street in Seaside, the community builds a combination public bath house, dune walk-over, and belvedere where the street meets the beach. Stuart Cohen and Anders Nereim began working at Seaside when the third street, East Ruskin Street, was completed. The design of the pavilion resulted from a fluid thinking that lies, according to the designers, somewhere between architecture and furniture, detail and structure. ". . . We passed sketches to each other without making distinctions between the disciplines. We thought of our favorite things, and went for that certain consistency of expression and detailing which seems to radiate from them."

Both the condominiums and the Avery Bed and Breakfast express an honesty of structure that is associated with the skeletal quality of wood construction. Both are designed within the constraints of the Type IV "antebellum mansion." Note the various interpretations of the mandatory two-story porch.

1

2

3   4

Avery Bed and Breakfast

Seaside Condominiums
1.
Front elevation
2.
Section
3.
First floor plan
4.
Second floor plan

Avery Bed and Breakfast
5.
Stair section
6.
Front elevation
7.
Side elevation
8–10.
First, second, and third floor plans

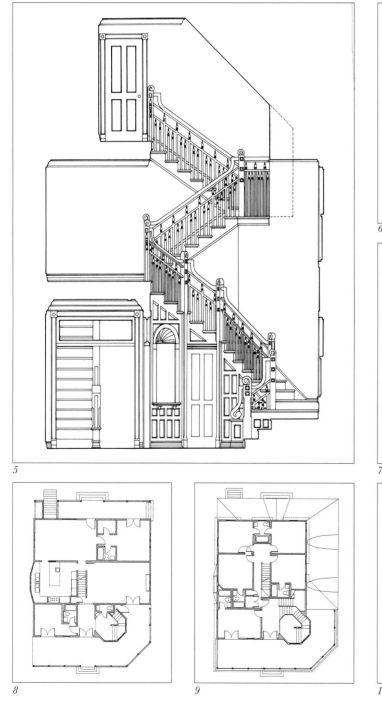

5

6

7

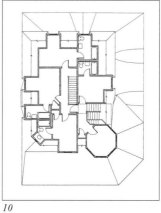

8

9

10

East Ruskin Street
Beach Pavilion

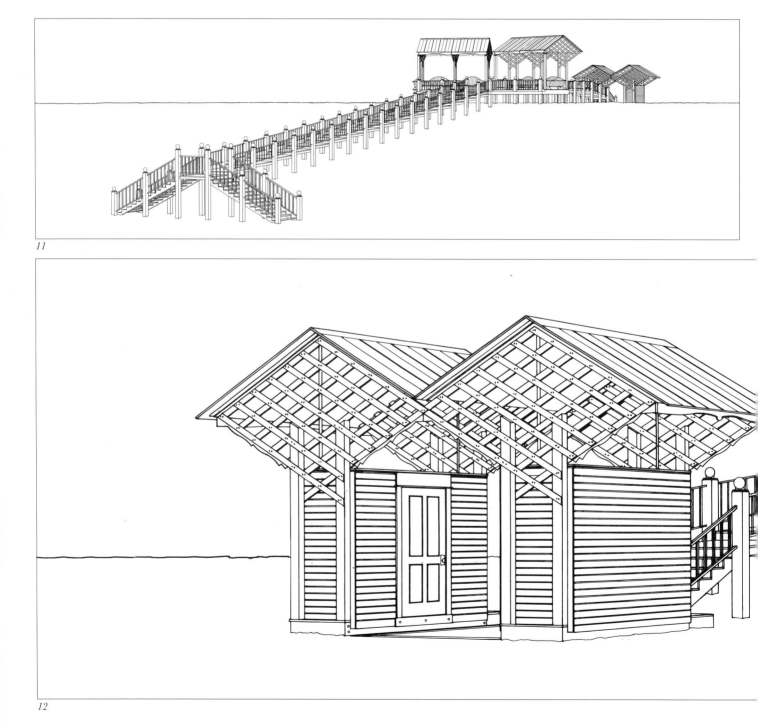

11

12

11.
Oblique elevation
12.
Perspective from street
13–14.
Sections and elevations

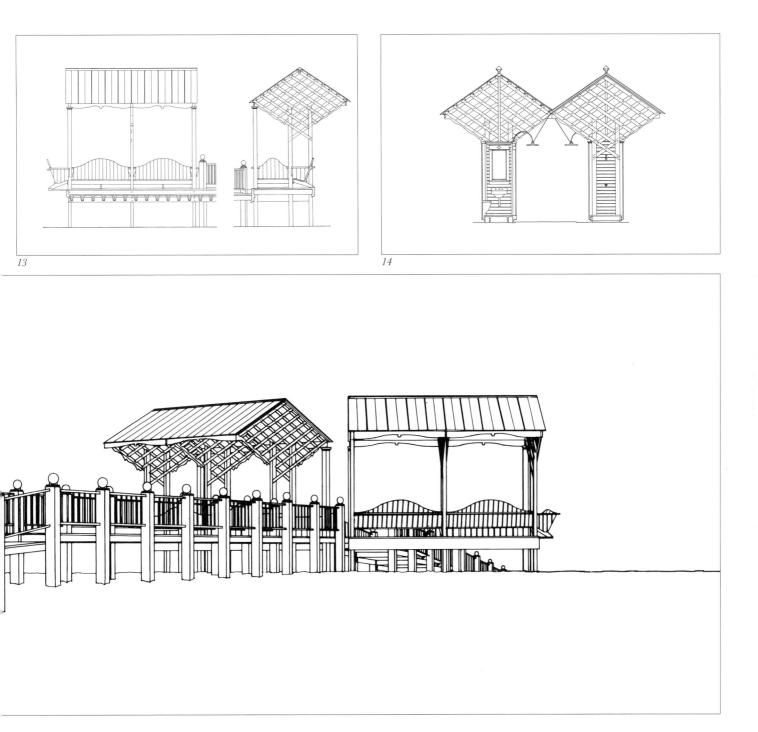

13

14

Leon Krier

Krier/Wolff House

Leon Krier is a self-taught architect who has been at the center of a recent reexamination of urban planning. His drawings and theory have been an important component of the architectural world for the last fifteen years, but he had not actually built a building until this house at Seaside, which was completed in 1989. Raised in Luxembourg, his understanding of traditional European urbanism continues a train of thought first articulated by Camillo Sitte in the late nineteenth century. Krier calls for the city to be pedestrian-scaled, built up by accretion, dense in its fabric, and understood through visual cues. As a mentor and unofficial consultant to Davis, Duany and Plater-Zyberk, he brought elements of this sensibility to the urban design of Seaside, most prominently through the suggestion of a series of pedestrian paths on the interiors of certain blocks.

In acknowledgement of his influence on the town plan, Krier was asked to design the tower for the central square at Seaside. No deadlines being given, Krier had the time to study the possibilities in dozens of sketches. Krier's own house is an indirect result of this commission. (He received the lot on which his house was built in lieu of a fee for the tower designs.) The house appears as an accretional assemblage of pieces, with porches and a tower added to a basic block of rooms. The double height living room is raised to the second floor as a piano nobile, with the bedroom on the ground floor and a study/tower on the top floor. Building details are often based on traditional stone construction, but executed in wood.

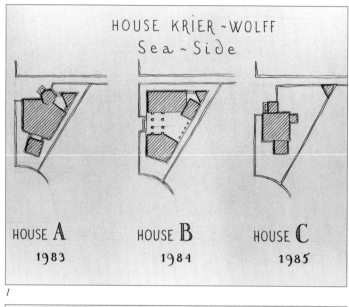

1

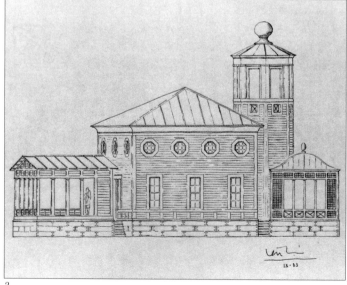

2

1.
Houses A–C, 1983–1985
Comparative site plans
2.
House A, 1983
Elevation

3–4.
House B, 1984
Axonometric sketches
5–6.
House C, 1985
Elevations

3

4

5

6

Krier/Wolff House

7

8

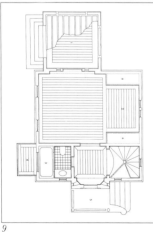

9

10

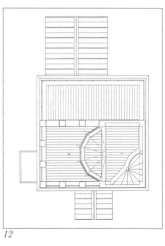

11

12

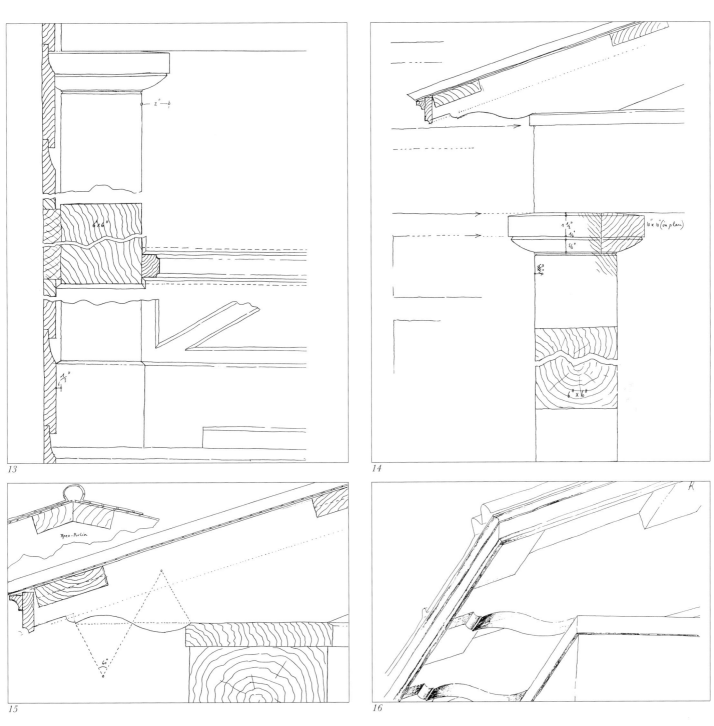

13

14

15

16

Krier/Wolff House

17

18

19

20

21

Town Hall

Church

22

23

Tower

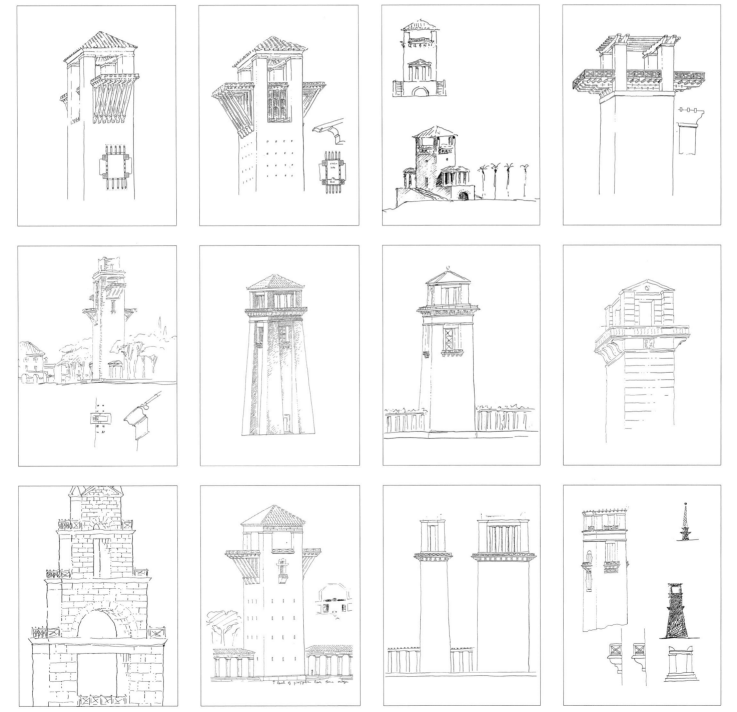

169

Tower

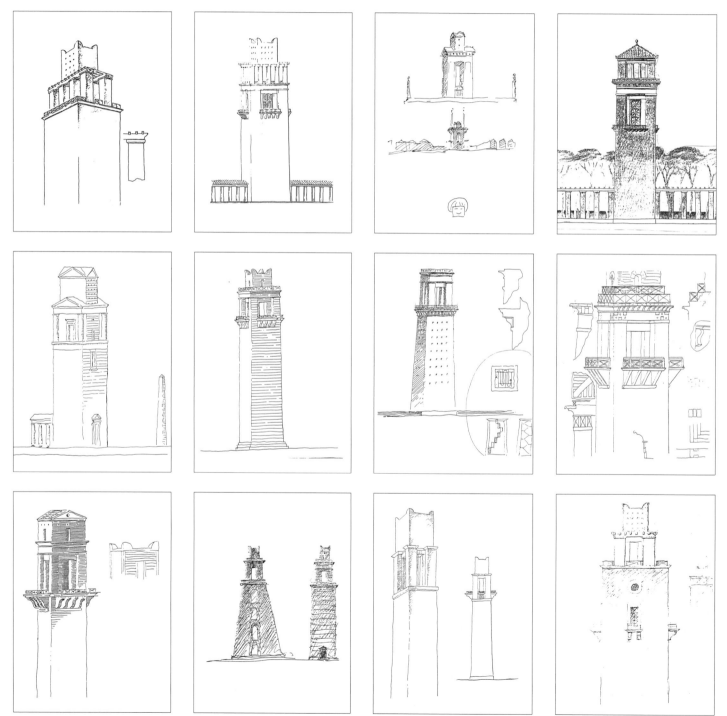

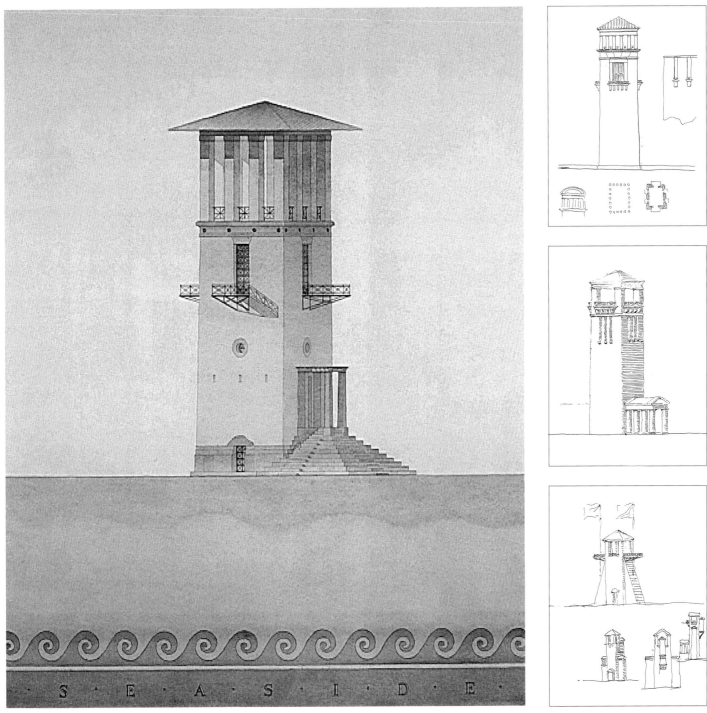

S · E · A · S · I · D · E ·

Steven Holl

Hybrid Building

Steven Holl's work at Seaside supports the initial wisdom of enlisting the contributions of a variety of architects in designing the town's buildings. He started work after roughly a third of the town had been built, and his commission was Seaside's first permanent building on the central square. The Hybrid Building incorporates commercial spaces on the ground floor, offices on the second, and apartments with a shared courtyard on the third and fourth levels. Holl's idiosyncratic architecture, including a written narrative which explained the disposition of its elements (e.g. apartments facing west, toward the setting sun, are for "boisterous types," while those facing the rising sun in the east are for particular "melancholic types": a tragic poet, a musician, and a mathematician) was in marked contrast to the surrounding buildings. The Hybrid Building's size, scale, and program, within the existing three-score residential structures flanking it at the time of its completion, significantly changed the perception of the town.

1

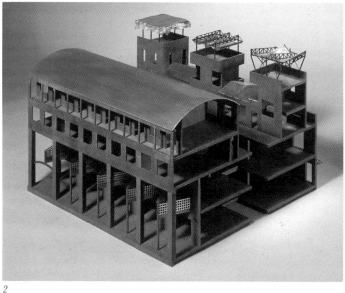

2

1.
Axonometric, watercolor
2.
Model
(Photo: Susan Wides)

3.
Exploded axonometric
4.
Section
5.
Third floor plan
6.
Fourth floor plan

3

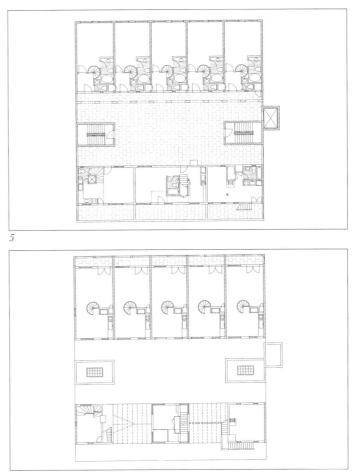

5

6

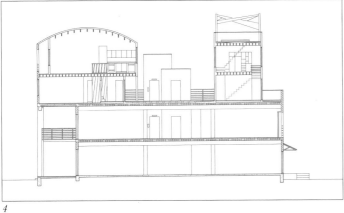

4

7

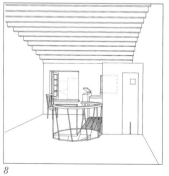

8

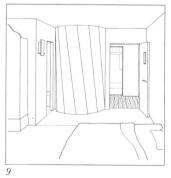

9

10.
View from town square
(Photo: Steven Brooke)

11–12.
House of the musician
Interior perspectives

13.
House of the mathemetician
Exterior perspective

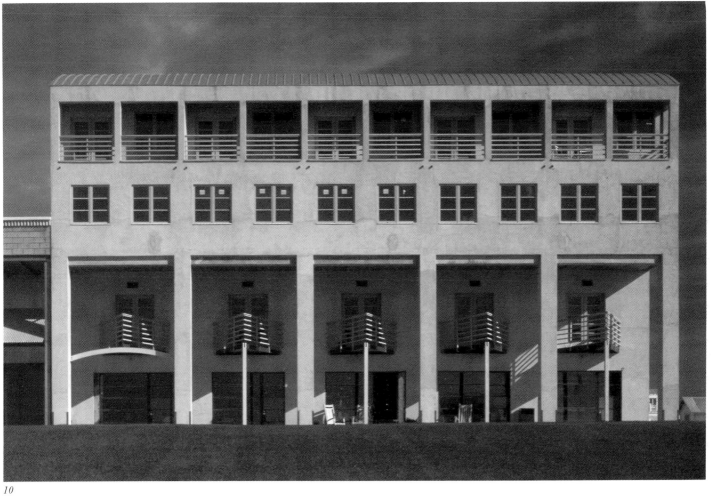

10

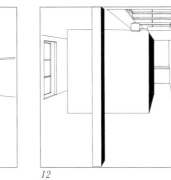

11

12

13

14

Walter Chatham

Chatham House

Walter Chatham has been involved with Seaside for many years, starting with his project for the Town Hall. The program is an interpretation of the conventional hotel program: a conference room is pulled out from the body of the hotel, allowing it to be used occasionally as a large meeting place for town citizens. The original urban plan had anticipated that this project would have steady cornice lines, in the manner of Jackson Square in New Orleans. Chatham instead chose to create a series of discrete but linked pavilions. The subsidiary pavilions have a flexible program and could potentially be used as school classrooms and offices for an institute devoted to research on town planning.

His own house has been one of Seaside's most controversial projects. By placing the "porch" between two pavilions (rather than using it as a more conventional buffer between house and street), and by using unusual finishes (silver paint and copper tubing), Chatham gives the house a brash, extroverted quality that has unsettled several of his neighbors. A variance was granted for the use of metal cladding on the walls, as well as on the roof, and for a 2 x 4 square foot grass "doormat." Chatham has also designed two Type III party-wall houses on Ruskin Square, in a modernist vernacular that complies fully with the codes. The mixed-use nature of the program (i.e. mandatory shop fronts on the first floor) requires a wasteful and unnecessary duplication of stairs, as prescribed by the Southern Standard Building Code, but both of Chatham's designs cleverly accommodate them.

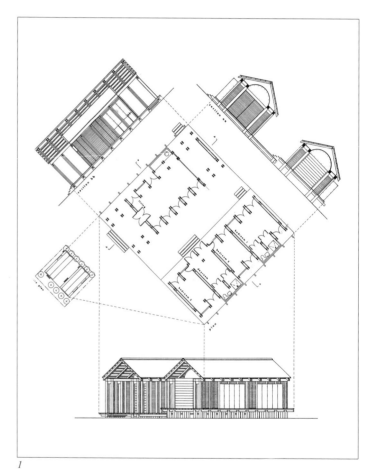

1

1.
*Composite drawing: plan,
sections, and elevation*
2.
View from Ruskin Street

3.
View from town center
4.
*Interior view
(Photos: Michael Moran)*

2

3

4

Town Hall

5

6

7.
Model, aerial view
8.
Model, view from town square
9.
Model, aerial view of Assembly Building

10.
Model, view of arcade
11.
Model, detail of Assembly Building
(Photos: Michael Moran)

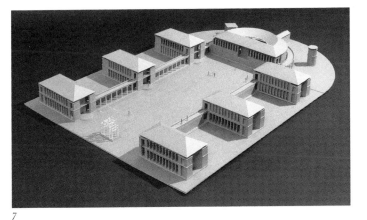

7

8

9

10

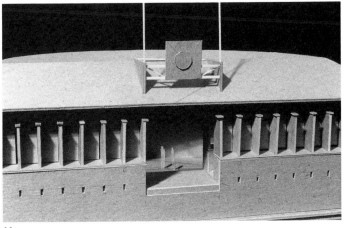

11

Meyer House

12.
View from foot path
(Photo: Michael Moran)
13.
Second floor plan

12

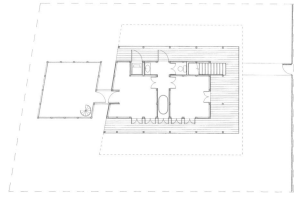

13

Forsythe
House

14.
Model elevation
(Photo: Michael Moran)
15.
First floor plan

Pugin
House

16.
Model elevation
(Photo: Michael Moran)
17.
Second floor plan

14

16

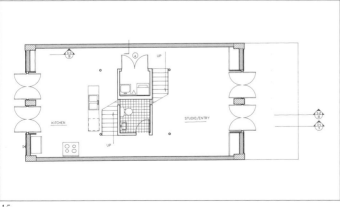

15

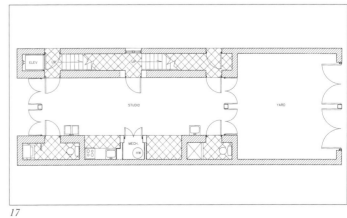

17

Joan Chan and David Mohney

Restaurant Pavilion

David Mohney was first involved with Seaside as a curator of the Seaside exhibition in New York. Mohney and his partner Joan Chan eventually designed a structure for the town. The pavilion is one of a collection of buildings surrounding the beachfront restaurant. Originally, it was also intended as a pavilion/clubhouse for Seaside residents living on east-west streets. There have been many schemes for the arrangement of these buildings at the water's edge. Chan and Mohney were inspired by one of Krier's drawings which pictured a heterogeneous collection of building geometries rendered as columnated, open air structures. Chan and Mohney's pavilion is distinguished by its pure geometry and precise interaction with light. It was intended as a small-town Pantheon with an oculus and "coffering" rendered in wood construction.

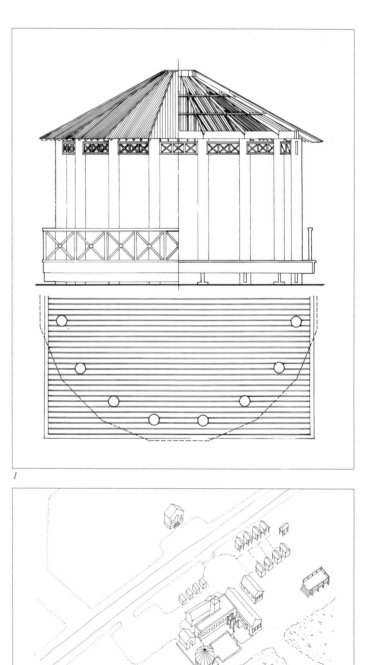

1

2

1.
*Composite drawing: plan,
section, and elevation*
2.
Site sketch
(Photo: Michael Moran)

3.
View from beach
4.
View from terrace
5.
View from street
(Photos: David Mohney)

6.
View through oculus
(Photo: Michael Moran)

3

4

6

5

Michael McDonough

Jefferson House

In his Jefferson House project, Michael McDonough pays homage to Thomas Jefferson's "cultural aspirations for America" by incorporating elements of the third president's designs and writings. The house was intended for a Type IV lot, but it does not meet the code, which requires that the entire frontage be colonnaded. It was intended to be an institutional building, which is one of the variety of programs, along with inns, apartment houses, and professional offices, that can be accommodated in this type. The Honeymoon Cottage project and West Ruskin Street beach pavilion draw upon several sources: the additive tradition in folk architecture, the American crafts tradition, and elements of Southern vernacular architecture, seen, perhaps, through a Venturi-esque lens.

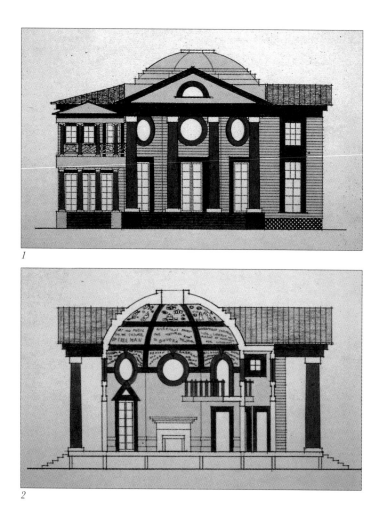

1

2

Honeymoon Cottage

Honeymoon Cottage
3–5.
Elevations

West Ruskin Street Beach Pavilion
6.
Model view, perspective from road
7.
Model view, detail of screen

West Ruskin Street Beach Pavilion

3

6

4

7

5

John Massengale

Dawson House

1.
*View from Route 30–A
(Photo: Michael Moran)*
2.
First floor plan

John Massengale served as Town Architect from 1985–1986. During this tenure, he toured small towns throughout the South, and was especially attracted to the ante-bellum houses. The Dawson house is built in a classical language which was not intended for private buildings at Seaside. Massengale, as both designer and Town Architect, granted himself the necessary variances that eliminated the overhang and allowed the use of the color white, which had been reserved for civic buildings. The possibility of constructing private buildings in the classical language was exploited quickly, and unexpectedly, by Leon Krier, Scott Merrill, and others.

The Atheneum is named after a hotel of the same name in Chautauqua, New York, and combines commercial and public spaces. An open, covered passage links the central square with Ruskin Square. The upper floors combine small two-story hotel apartment units, and a grand public room.

1

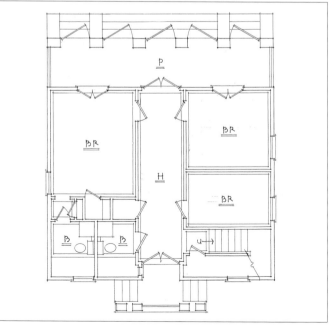

2

Atheneum Hotel

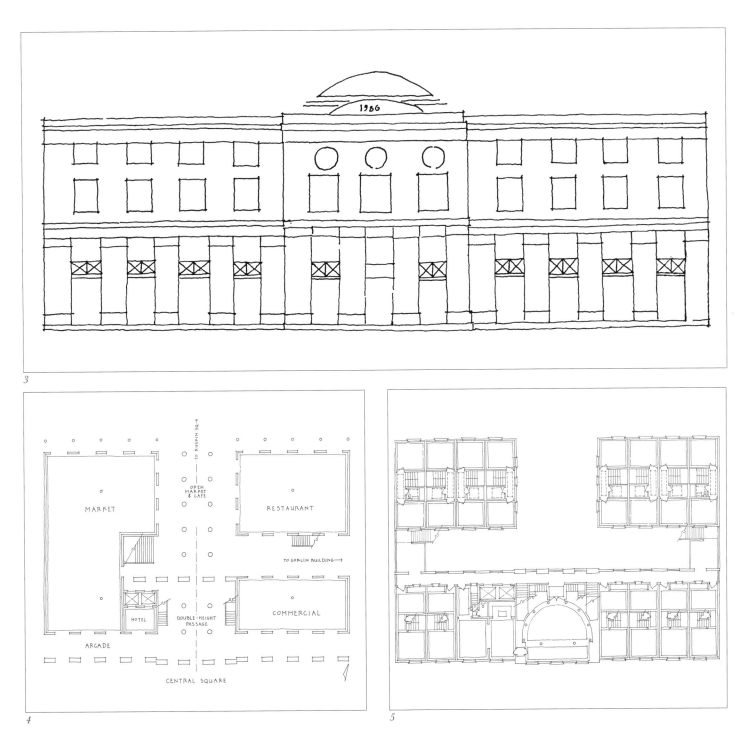

3.
Elevation
4.
First floor plan
5.
Second floor plan

3

4

5

Alex Gorlin

Leake House

1.
Model
(Photo: Alex Gorlin)

Alex Gorlin was one of the first architects to design a project for the town center. Gorlin's work begins with an assumption about the primacy of the site as a generator of architectural form. The town center building is intended to relate the commercial center to the residential streets by forming a gate where Seaside Avenue enters the central square. This gate also frames the view to the pool pavilion at the far end of the avenue. The building combines the required shop front on its lower floor with the seemingly detached residential elements on its upper floors. The Leake House is one of the first structures to test the row house typology (Type III) designated for Ruskin Square.

1

Town Center Building

2.
Axonometric
3.
Perspective view towards town square
4.
First floor plan
5.
Second floor plan

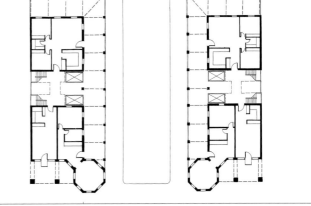

2

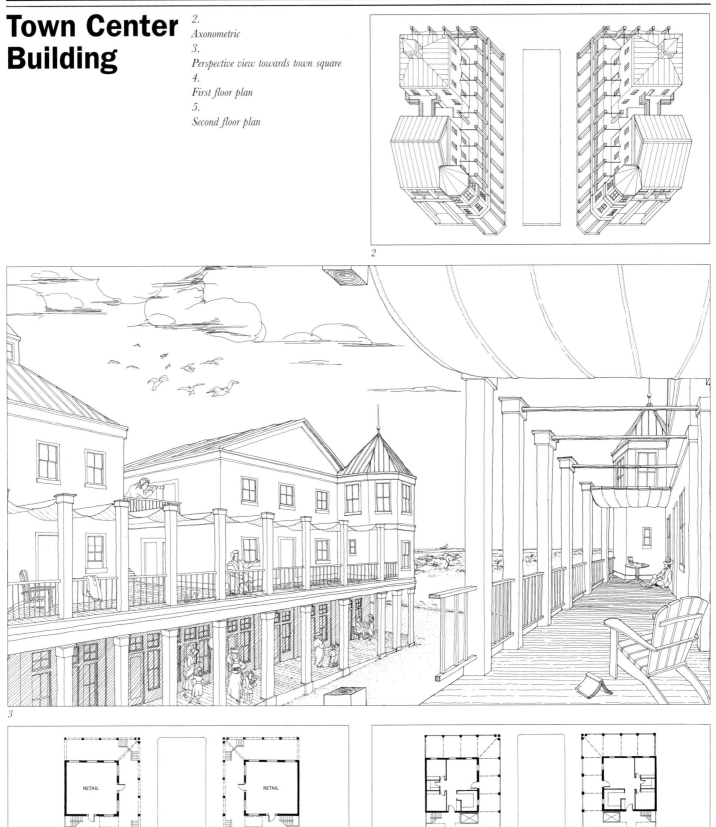

3

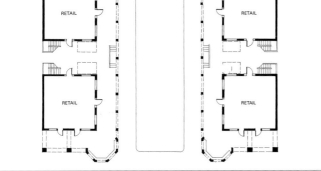

4

5

Anthony Ames

Crews House

This project was commissioned during the mid-1980s. During this period, new attempts were being made to interpret the code with less concern for the stylistic elements of historical prototype. The plan is molded by the urban requirements of the site. This is a Type V house with the mandatory two-story open porch to the street. This house meets the code in every detail: flat roofs are permitted as long as they are habitable; windows are vertical or square (although ganged up to form horizontals). The house responds to its site with an "L" shape, relating both to the foot path and to the formal qualities of the street. In addition, the "L" provides an interior, private enclosure, and an effective distribution of public and private spaces within the plan. The Crews House draws on modern antecedents while fulfilling code requirements; however, the clients preferred a more traditional building and the project was not executed.

1

2

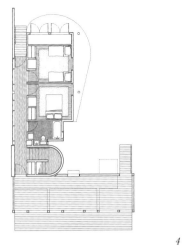

1.
Site plan
2.
Perspective from Seaside Avenue
3.
First floor plan
4.
Second floor plan
5.
Perspective from garden

3   4

5

Victoria Casasco

Appell House

Victoria Casasco was part of the initial urban design charrette and acted as Town Architect in 1987. She designed buildings in the town that attempted to test the limits of the code by diverging from typical interpretations and introducing modern operations of space making. The Appell House abstracts typical Southern vernacular practices regarding wood construction. The structural skeleton is exposed and the wood cladding is treated as an exterior "skin." Also, the transparency between the interior and exterior provides for complex spatial relationships, while responding to local climate. This house and the other building projects also explore experimental uses of materials. Casasco's work is among that of several designers who have demonstrated that the architectural code is potentially quite expansive with regard to architectural intent.

1

2

3

1.
Side view
(Photo: Victoria Casasco)
2.
Exploded axonometric

3.
Longitudinal elevation
(Photo: Victoria Casasco)
4.
View of roof terrace
(Photo: Keller Easterling)
5–6.
Sections and elevations

4

5

6

Walton–Dufuniak Library

Bud and Alley's Oyster Bar

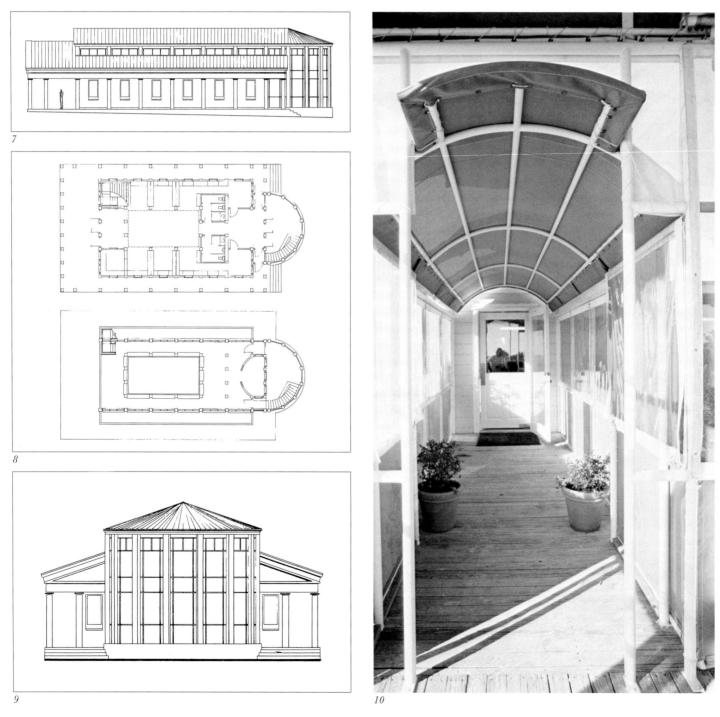

7

8

9

10

11

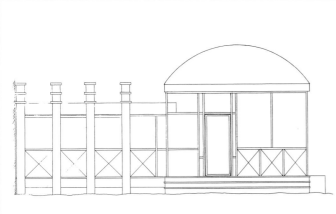

12

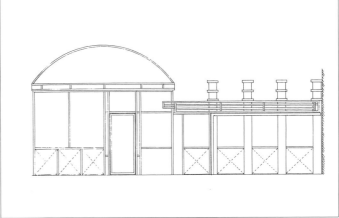

13

Cooper Johnson Smith **Cooper House I**

Elements of seaside architecture from different regions of the United States, not just the Southeast, are used by this Tampa-based firm to create playful, evocative structures. For example, the tower of the Cooper House is manipulated into a widow's walk, typical of northeastern houses. Like many of Seaside's public amenities, the individually crafted playground structures are seemingly incidentally disposed in the public realm. (The garden architecture in Rosewalk is another example.) The firm also assisted with construction documentation for Krier's house.

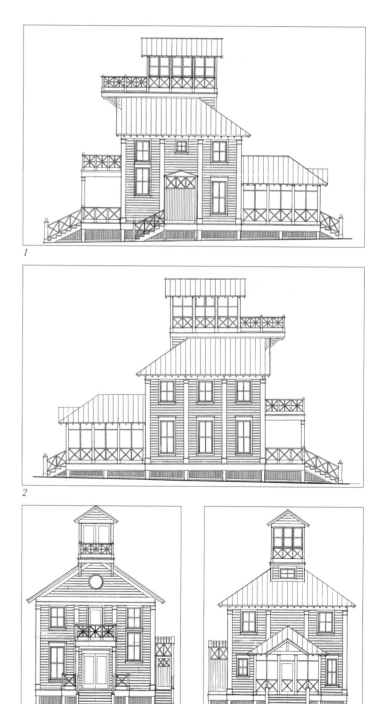

1

2

3

4

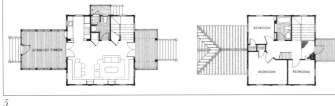

5

1–4.
Elevations
5.
Plans (clockwise from top left):
roof, third, second, and
first floor
6.
View from Tupelo Circle
(Photo: Steven Brooke)
7.
View from pedestrian walkway
(Photo: Cooper Johnson Smith)

7

6

Landscape Follies

8.
Playground bridge, plan and elevation
9.
Seesaw elevation

Cooper House II

10.
Front elevation
11.
Side elevation

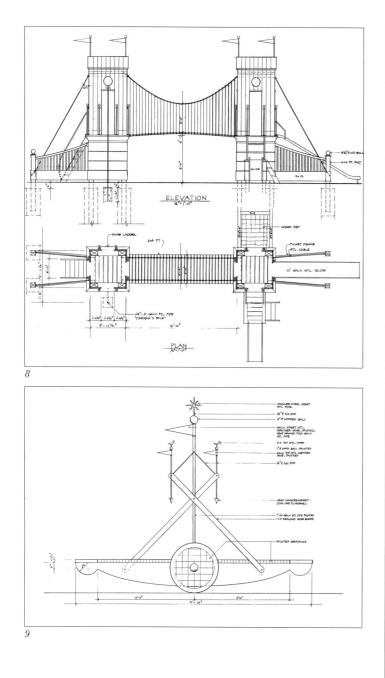

8

9

10

11

Raeburn House

12

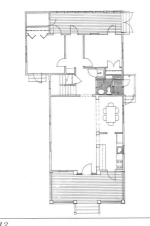

13

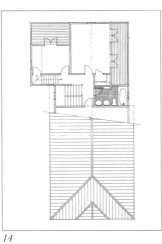

14

15

Victor Bowman

Fritze House

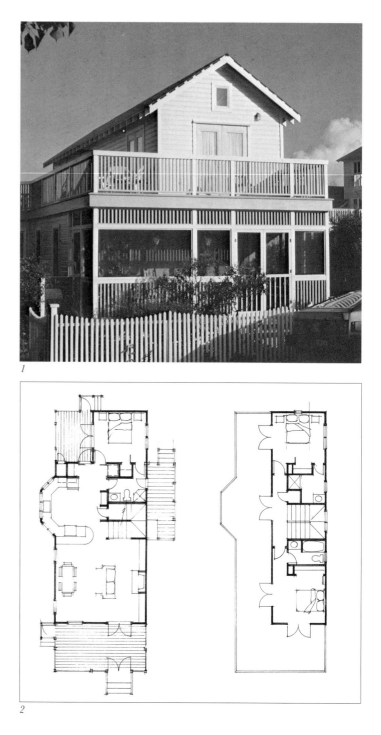

1.
View from pedestrian path
(Photo: Victor Bowman)
2.
First and second floor plans

Victor Bowman first came to Seaside to design a cottage for his own family. Eventually he built both an office and a residence in the town, and has maintained a successful design/build practice there for six years. Bowman developed a technique of designing open, fluid spaces in plan which simultaneously respect the basic massing of the Southern vernacular house and remain within the requirements of the code. He developed those plans into a variety of types that he reinterprets for different clients. Bowman is also one of the first architects working on Type III row houses for Ruskin Square.

1

2

Ruskin Square Town Houses

Bed and Breakfast

Mustachio House

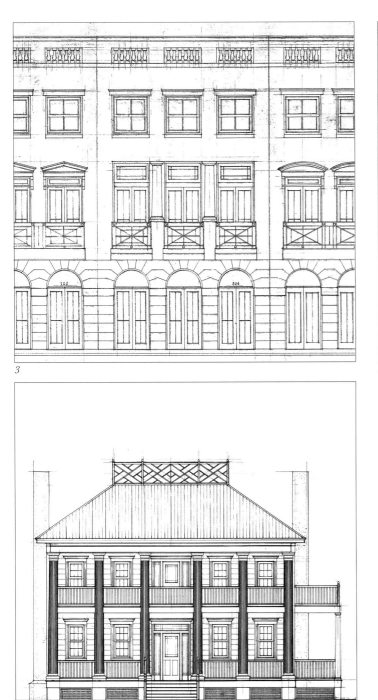

3

5

4

203

Steve Badanes

Natchez Street Beach Pavilion

1.
Site plan sketch
2.
Perspective sketch

The urban designers anticipated that, in a few instan-cesd, some architects would take on both the design and the construction of buildings at Seaside. This is the first beach pavilion to be carried out in this manner. Unlike many designer/builders, Badanes does not base his practice in one locale; he typically takes on one project at a time, moving to the site and devoting his full energies to both its design and construction. The Natchez Street beach pavilion places an oversized wooden beach umbrella on the crest of the dune to mark the end of the street and its linkage with the beach.

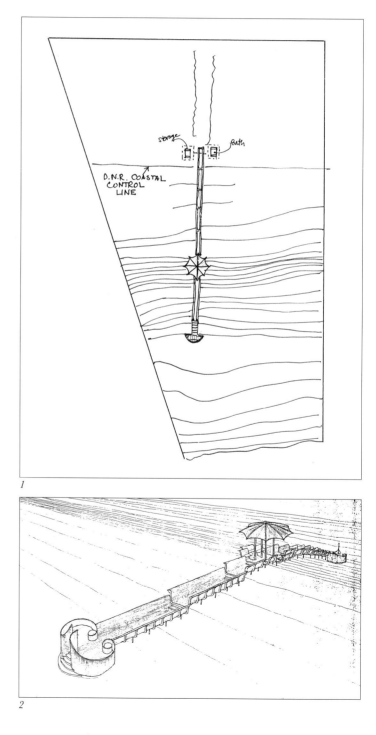

1

2

Rafael Pelli

Dowler/Settle House

For Rafael Pelli, the massing of a typical Florida Panhandle house is designed to receive light and shadow in particular ways. The Dowler/Settle House is a composition of simple volumes with varied surfaces. A dark wood shake-gable roof gives a strong profile against the sky and terminates the diagonal street vista. The slotted-gable end changes to screen porch and then to solid siding, thereby manipulating the light and shadows that enter the house. By creating a progression from dark to light, these surfaces help define a gradation of the spaces of the house as well, from top to bottom, back to front, and inside to outside.

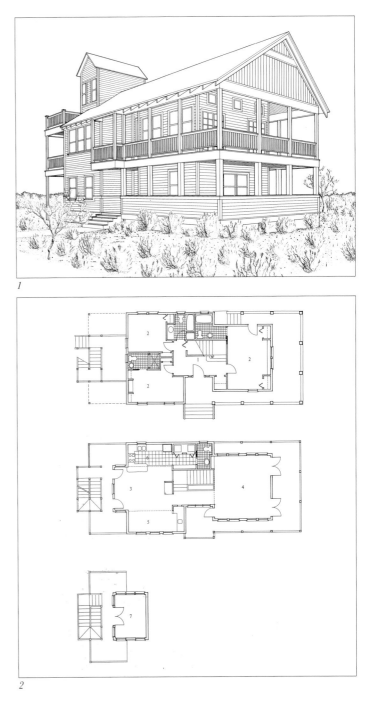

1

2

Tony Atkin

Pensacola Street Beach Pavilion

Owing to the height of the dune at the foot of Pensacola Street, this beach pavilion is among the most prominent at Seaside. It gives the appearance of a tempietto set on a rusticated base. The diagrammatic rustication of the base and plastic sea gull/weather vane gesture to the regional popular culture (especially the honky-tonk beach life of Panama City, fifteen miles to the west) and perhaps to another Philadelphia architect, Robert Venturi, who continues to be an exponent of the place of popular culture in contemporary American architecture.

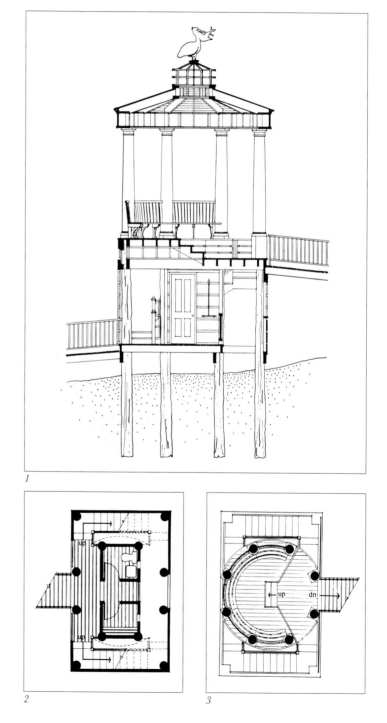

1

2

3

Roger Ferri

Odessa Street Beach Pavilion

Exempt from code restrictions, public buildings like the beach pavilions invite a number of different kinds of expression just as they invite recreation on the beach. Rather than making historical allusion, Roger Ferri's Odessa Street Beach Pavilion evokes a variety of experiences of life by the ocean. Ferri says, "It is a capriccio on vernacular 'stick' construction, in which the diagonal wind brace is raised to the level of the generative motif. It is a sand comber's shack, whose spare economy of means expresses the littoral freedom from worldly encumbrances. It is a tropical palm-frond hut whose abstracted 'sheathing' alludes to the Caribbean Palmetto frond of the dunes. It is a Chippendale fretwork porch that creates shifting kaleidoscopic effects; solid from some angles, it dematerializes from others into a flickering tent of sea and sky."

1

208

1.
View from beach
(Photo: Steven Brooke)
2.
Sketch of interior

Scott Merrill

Corker House

1.
View from street
2.
View from side
(Photos: Katherine Gallaway)
3.
First and second floor plans

Scott Merrill served as Town Architect from 1988–1990, the longest period of any of the seven people who have held the position. Through the repetition of simple structures, Merrill attempted to create background buildings that defer to the urban space rather than stand·alone as objects. The buildings combine fine classical detail with the plain and austere qualities of many American small-town buildings.

Merrill's designs are varied in program, ranging from the Honeymoon Cottages (Type V) to the Motor Court (Type III) to a variety of house types. The Honeymoon Cottages include both building design as well as site planning. The Ruskin Square town house study proposes that each group of five row houses be designed by a single architect. The result was convincing, but the sequence of building by individual owners could not be co-ordinated, and thus the buildings are being individually designed. The Motor Court was a hybrid program containing a parking lot and a storage warehouse in a "dogtrot" pattern. The planners had anticipated that these units would permit people to build smaller houses while retaining possessions in a storage space, a common situation among newly retired people.

1

2

3

Hultquist House

4

6

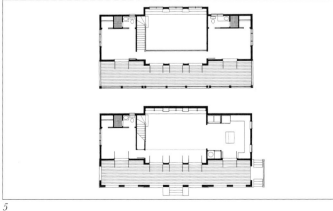

5

7

Honeymoon Cottages

8

9

8.
View from beach
9.
View from porch
10.
View from Route 30–A

11.
Plan and elevations
(Photos: Steven Brooke)
12.
Ensemble view of cottages from
pedestrian walkway

10

12

11

Williams House

16.
View from the beach
(Photo: Scott Merrill)
17.
Axonometric
18.
First floor plan
19.
Second floor plan

16

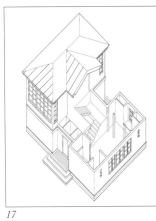

17

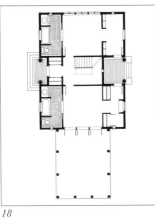

18

19

Hinton
House

Doyle
Cottage

20

24

21

25

22   23

26   27

Johnson House

Motor Court and Mini Storage

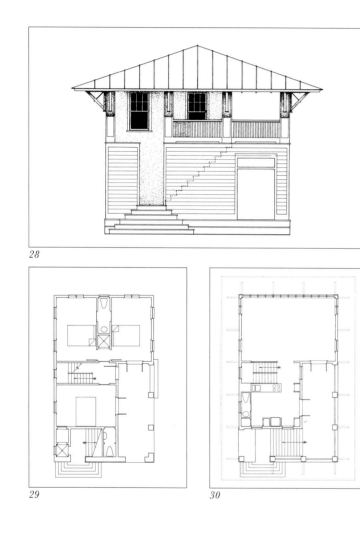

28

29

30

31

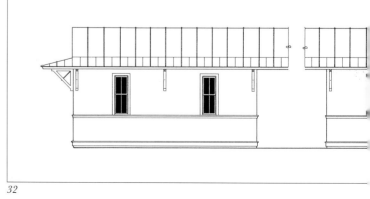

32

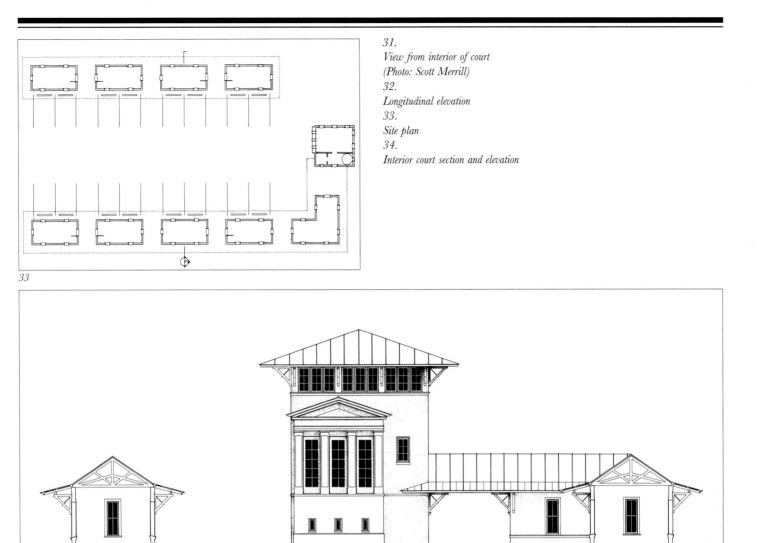

33

31.
View from interior of court
(Photo: Scott Merrill)
32.
Longitudinal elevation
33.
Site plan
34.
Interior court section and elevation

34

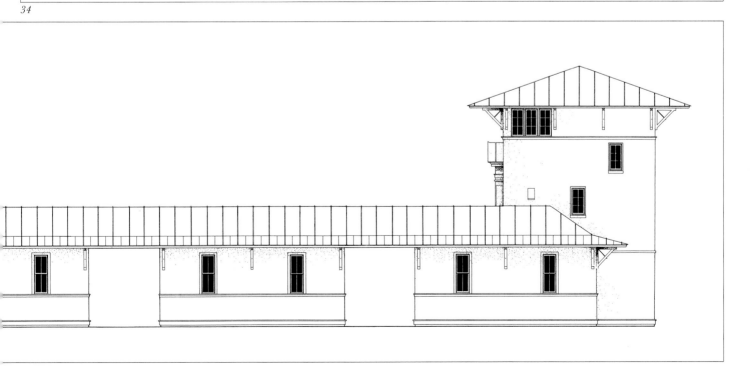

Roberto Behar

Motel Rooms

Roberto Behar's projects for Seaside mine the most fundamental aspects of a building for their experiential power. The Motel Rooms were developed around the idea of travel, evoking emotions associated with movement and memories—of the happiness of the arrival and the melancholy of the departure. Part of their inspiration is derived from paintings like Edward Hopper's *Western Motel* (p. 248) or *Compartment C* and from films like *La Strada* by Federico Fellini. The Motel Rooms can be sited in a variety of arrangements.

In the "non-denominational temple" Behar relies on the contrast between the experience of the exterior and the experience of the interior spatial and sectional qualities. Behar says, "The exterior associates itself in tension with the classical, the industrial, and the new form of the vernacular; while the interior, with the sacred as a reference, is open towards the sky. Brick, steel, and wood on the exterior and white stucco and stone in the interior support both American and spiritual climates."

1

2

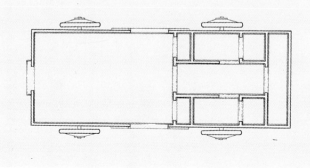

3

Temple

4

5

6

Charles Barrett

Pool House

Charles Barrett has been involved in drawing perspective renderings of various Seaside projects and other Duany/Plater-Zyberk town-planning projects. The pool house is Barrett's own project for Seaside. The design proposes a ritualized version of the Seaside vernacular by situating the building within a classical, even mythological, context. Barrett has explored connections between classical proportions and those resulting from vernacular types, recognizing the correspondence between the intense repetition of details typical in wood construction and the dentils and entablature in the primitive Ionic order. The building is oriented toward the setting sun with a view to the water, town, and a stand of oak trees at the edge of the site. At the end of the day, the setting sun reflects in the lap pool under a mural depicting Apollo resting in the grottos of Tethys.

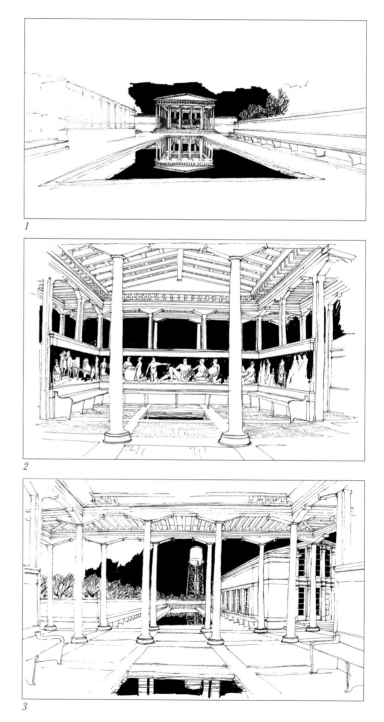

1

2

3

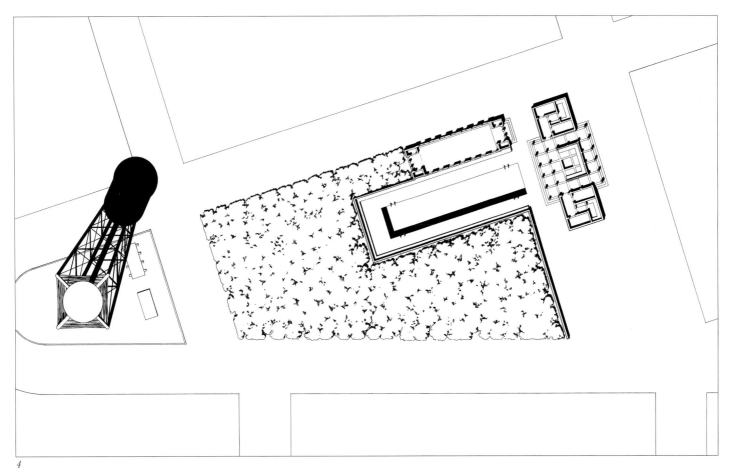

4

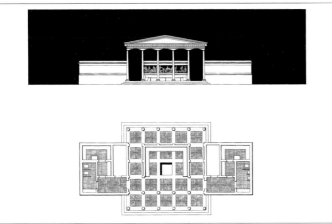

5

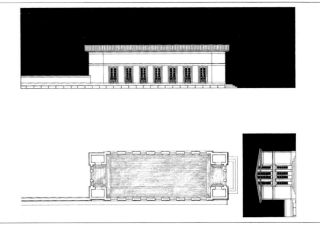

6

Luis Trelles

Ruskin Square
Town House

Luis Trelles was a member of the original urban design team working that developed the Seaside town plan. This is his first architectural project for the town. While many urban Southern types are influenced by French, Spanish, and English styles, Trelles's Ruskin Square town house design is a new hybrid of regional and Spanish architecture.

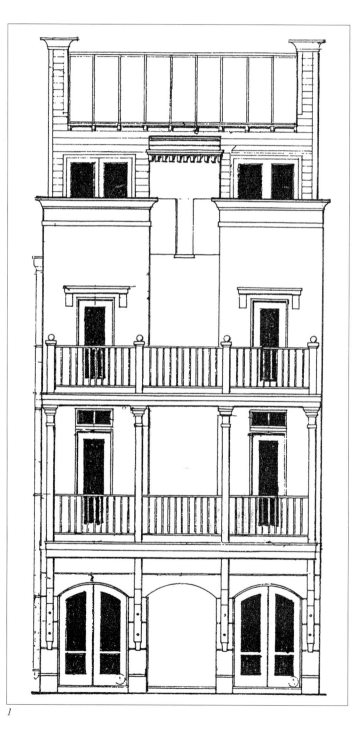

1

1.
Front elevation
2.
Oblique elevation

3.
Side elevation
4.
Section

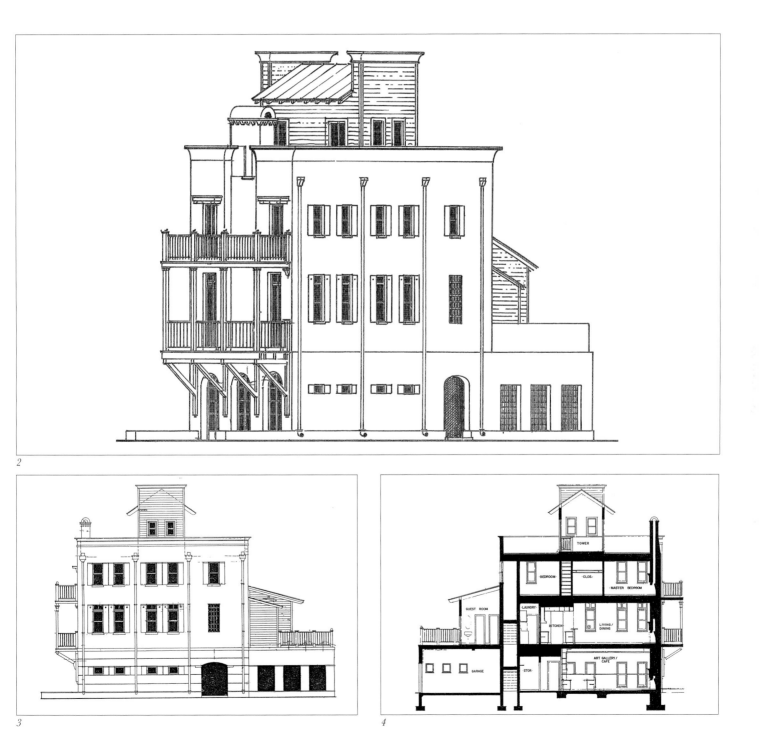

2

3

4

225

David Coleman

Pavilion

This obelisk is designed to be one of two beach entries at the east and west ends of the central square. Switchback ramps provide handicapped access through the dunes to the beach. The designer, who studied in Copenhagen, characterizes this pavilion as a "primordial form" distilled from earlier designs that were inspired by images of northern classicism in Scandinavian architecture.

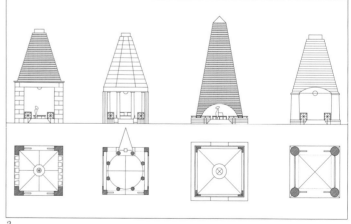

1

2

1.
Perspective
2.
Elevations and plans
3.
Section and roof plan

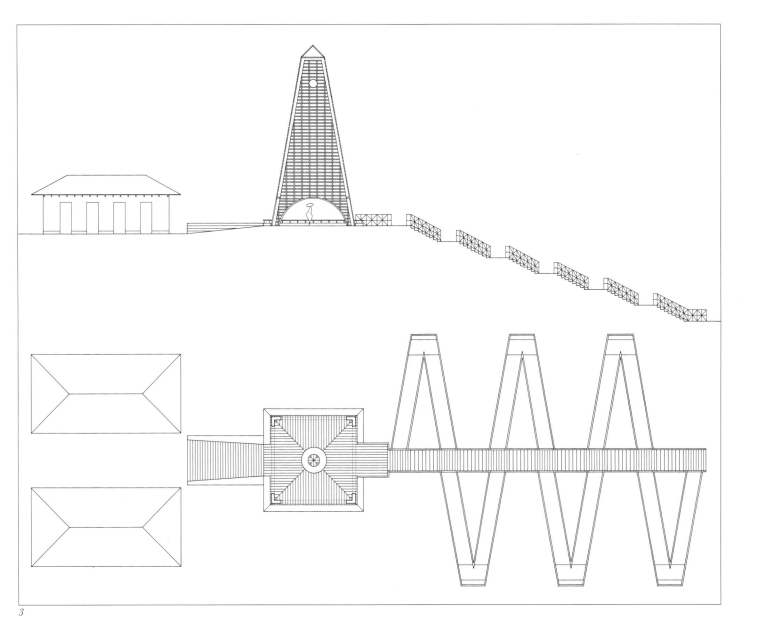

3

Rodolfo Machado and Jorge Silvetti

Downtown Building

Programmatically, this building is identical to the Hybrid Building by Steven Holl, and is sited directly across from it on the central square. In contrast to Holl's idiosyncratic resolution of the program with its lyrical narrative, Rodolfo Machado and Jorge Silvetti have distilled the prototype to a level of sparse clarity. Although located on the public square, the commercial buildings are not restricted to white exteriors (like the public buildings), and Machado and Silvetti have introduced a polychrome exterior to the project. A courtyard at the residential level provides a semi-public area for the apartments, with a framed view over the central square.

1

2

228

1.
*View of the garden/terrace from
the interior courtyard*
2.
Section

3.
South elevation
4.
Third floor plan
5.
View of courtyard

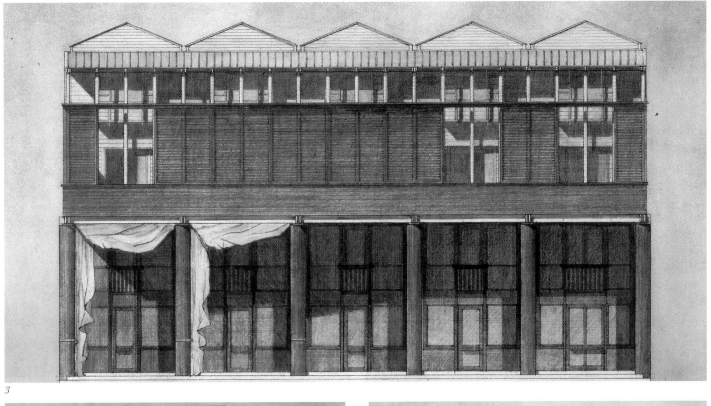

3

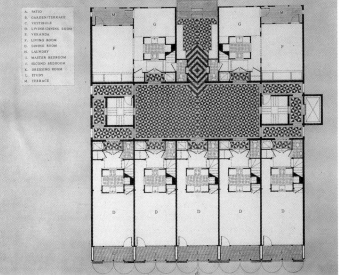

4

5

229

Landscape Designs

Douglas Duany served as an unofficial landscape architect during Seaside's early years. He was among the first to advocate nurturing and refining the existing flora rather than replacing it with typically suburban shrubs and grasses. He studied the site extensively, noting the locations of significant groupings of shrubs and trees. In some cases the decision to preserve these areas necessitated the resiting of some houses, and variances were granted to the setback requirements of the code.

1

1.
Corner garden
2.
Seaside gardens
(Photos: Duany/Plater-Zyberk)

2

Selected Houses

A number of people with no formal design training have chosen to take on the design responsibility for houses at Seaside, following the provisions of the urban and architectural codes. Some are builders who originally worked on projects designed by others, but then chose to execute their own designs; some are individuals who designed their own houses, and then took on other projects speculatively. In almost all cases, this work was carried out by people living in Seaside, looking firsthand at the town-in-progress for ideas and inspiration. This was to be the standard working method at Seaside, in Duany and Plater-Zyberk's original conception of the town, and historically there is a great precedent for it in nineteeth- and twentieth-century American towns. Indeed, much of the graphic simplicity and clarity of the urban code developed by the town planners was intended from the outset to assist people working in this way.

These houses are extremely important for a variety of reasons. In contrast to some house designs that have been highly profiled, these buildings are more than just variations on a theme. They begin to make the town's fabric, deferring attention to the urban spaces and the street rather than to individual houses. In later phases of growth, they indicate how the new buildings of the town can expand upon initial designs. Furthermore, where a conventional development might have three or four house types with only a few permitted variations, Seaside allows each house type to be built out uniquely. As a result, slight variations between similar designs become the basis for a refined visual perception of the town and its houses; both trained and untrained observers of architecture at Seaside look more closely at the buildings there.

For example, Louis Hiett has built five houses at Seaside, which are all characterized by good proportions and an appropriate austerity that has eluded some trained designers. His own house exhibits great siting skills: it maintains the street corner on which it sits, and uses its porch to terminate the axis of a third street which intersects the plot at an oblique angle.

Suellen Hudson has built four houses, three of which have been refinements of a single type. Peter Horn, a builder-turned designer, looked to early Deborah Berke houses in planning the Horn/Hodges house. Benoit Laurent and Mark Breaux came to Seaside as builders, and after building several houses, each turned his attention to design, as well as construction.

A variety of projects conceived and carried out in this manner follow.

Hudson Houses

1.
102 East Ruskin Street
View from East Ruskin Street and
Route 30–A
2.
110 Odessa Street
View from Odessa Street

3.
115 Forest Street
View from Forest Street
4.
109 Pensacola Street
View from Pensacola Street
(Photos: David Mohney)
Suellen Hudson
Designer/Owner

1

2

3

4

Horn/Hodges House

5.
View from Forest Street
6.
View from Tupelo Street
(Photos: Peter Horn)
7.
First floor plan
Peter Horn
Builder/Designer

5

6

7

Breaux House

8–9.
Views from Butler Street
(Photos: David Mohney)
Mark Breaux
Designer/Builder/Owner

Wilkins House

10.
View from West Ruskin Street
(Photo: David Mohney)
Brad and Heidi Wilkins
Designers/Owners

8

9

10

Murray
House

11.
View from Forest Street
(Photo: David Mohney)
Bill Murray
Designer/Owner

Ashley
House

12.
View from street
(Photo: David Mohney)
Louis Hiett
Designer/Developer

11

12

11.
View from Forest Street
(Photo: David Mohney)

Scottie's House
Hiett House

13.
Scottie's House
View from street
(Photo: David Mohney)
Louis Hiett
Designer/Developer

14.
Hiett House
View from Seaside Avenue
(Photo: Louis Hiett)
15.
Hiett House
View from East Ruskin Street
(Photo: David Mohney)
Louis Hiett
Designer/Developer

13

14

15

Laurent Houses

16.
Laurent House I
View from Savannah Street
(Photo: David Mohney)
Benoit Laurent
Designer/Builder/Owner

17–18.
Laurent House II
View from Forest Street
(Photos: David Mohney)
Scott Merrill, Architect with
Benoit Laurent, Builder

16

17

18

Cone House

19.
Cone House
View from Odessa Street
(Photo: David Mohney)
Benoit Laurent, Designer/Builder
John and Jersey Cone, Owners

19

Neil Levine

Questioning the View: Seaside's Critique of the Gaze of Modern Architecture

Petrarch, about 1327, climbed Mont Ventoux near Avignon. He was accompanied by the belief that the view from the top would be significant, and unaccompanied by his friends, who saw no reason to go. Petrarch was right for six hundred years, and now his friends are right.

Donald Judd, *Arts Magazine* (March 1962)

Seaside can be read in many ways—as a proposition about urban design, as a discourse on developer/architect relations, as an argument for the vernacular, as a descriptive account of a place, as a demonstration of the increasing role of women in the architectural profession, as an essay on resort culture, or as a critique of modernism. In the course of this essay, I shall hope to touch on some, though certainly not all, of these, but it is Seaside's critique of what I am calling "the gaze of modern architecture" that will structure my reading.

Unlike most modern developments, especially those for resort communities, Seaside does not offer itself as the purchase of a view (fig. 1). In this, it goes against the common perception of not only what a modern vacationer expects, but also what modern architecture in general is supposed to provide. While the graphic means used to represent this economy of desire in a typical advertisement for an apartment in the up-scale real-estate section of the *New York Times Magazine* might be just market-driven and theoretically unsophisticated (fig. 2), the conceptual model to which they ultimately refer makes us acutely aware of the authority of "the view" in the aesthetics and culture of modernism (fig. 3). What Seaside provides, by contrast, is an ambience, an evocation of a place rather than simply its appropriation through visual means. Sense and memory are appealed to reciprocally. The key to its atmosphere is the binary relation between town and sea, perfectly characterized by the name Seaside.

The town lies beside the sea, well above it, linking it to the woods behind (p. 105). The bright white sand of the beach and the greenish-blue water of the gulf are masked from view by the high dune paralleling the

1.
*Advertisement for Aston Royal Sea
Cliff Resort, Pleasant Hawaiian
Holidays.* Independent Hawaii
(1989).
2.
Advertisement for Central Park Place.
New York Times Magazine
(18 March 1990).

main road. Periodically, the town steps over the dune and down to the beach through light-filled, festive pavilions that line the road and create, as it were, public thresholds to the sea (p. 76).

There is no fudging of boundaries at Seaside—no acculturation of nature, no naturalization of culture. For residents and visitors, it is a place of charm and gentleness, of pedestrian-scaled movement, and of close-grained community interaction. It is a townscape that comes as close as one might imagine possible today to the eighteenth-century classical ideal of "variety within unity"—somewhere between the University of Virginia and Chaux. A lucid geometric street pattern underlies and gives order to the playful detailing and pastel colors of the individual buildings. Towers of all shapes and types, some like temples, others more like tempiet-tos, become confused from a distance in the silvery blue plane of galvanized tin roofs that reflect the sky and provide a metallic base to the green cordon of trees that define the edge of the town, much as the scrub-topped dune defines the edge the beach.

When members of the architectural establishment, be they practitioners, critics, or educators, are asked their opinion, however, Seaside is usually described in more "problematic" terms. Known essentially through pictures, especially the early, high-keyed ones by Steven Brooke, the town is easily reduced to the image of the picturesque suburb, cozy and domesticated, its architectural character ruled by a very debatable "nostalgia" and historicism. In spite of that, the town-planning strategy is quite often acknowledged as a valid return to sound, community-based principles that should really only be evaluated if and when they are applied

to more "serious" purposes than a mere vacation resort. Thus reduced to the status of a model, Seaside is decontextualized. The very atmosphere it is all about is lost sight of in the distinction of form from content.

A relatively subtle extension of this critical position has begun to make itself felt with the recent completion and publication of Walter Chatham's house and Deborah Berke's and Steven Holl's buildings on the main square. Deliberately pushing the Seaside architectural code to accommodate an explicitly modern, even neomodernist vocabulary and esthetic, these structures have made "strong" and "tough" statements that have been read by eager critics as offering "reassuring evidence that the town's soundly drafted design rules need not promote an excess of 'cuteness' or 'mandate historicism.'"[1] The designers of the town itself, Andres Duany and Elizabeth Plater-Zyberk, have been reluctant to take a firm stand on this issue, maintaining that the structural rules they laid down in the urban code of Seaside are elastic enough to permit such wide divergences in style while still ensuring the urbanity and community atmosphere so clearly represented by the classical or vernacular buildings that devolve more logically and directly from the code.

All of which brings me to my main point, which is that despite whatever misgivings or questions have since been raised in the minds of its planners and architects, the conception of Seaside represents one of the most thoroughgoing and integral critiques of the ideology of modern architecture realized so far either in the United States or in Europe, and that its significance as a critique depends on the intimate fit of form and content defined by the design codes of the town. The

3

target is the fundamental privatization of experience in modern architecture with its corollary valorization of that which can be rendered in purely visual terms. The questioning of other essential values of modernism, such as the role of the author-architect, the belief in originality, and the hypostatization of space, all follow from this. The logic of the argument, as adumbrated by Duany and Plater-Zyberk, moves through a series of frames of reference, each one implying the next. First there is the Code, then the Street, and finally the Window, the interface of public and private where vision is defined in both its social and psychological dimensions.

Let me begin by saying something about the concept of a code. Codes are rarely, if ever, discussed in the history of modern architecture. One usually thinks of bureaucratic documents detailing wind loads, fire resistance, building-height setbacks, handicapped access, etc. To be sure, architects have begun more and more to discuss the growing importance of such restrictions in actually determining design decisions. But the mythology of modern architecture, whether it be based on Le Corbusier defying the "authorities" at Pessac or Marseilles, or Wright going to court in New York over the Guggenheim, is that building codes are philistine devices designed to thwart the individual creativity of the architect. No more so would this be the case than when a code for a small town has been drawn up to mandate a certain style.

From the point of view of modern architecture, building codes are simply unnecessary and unwelcome restraints. They inhibit the free play of the author's imagination and impede the search for "originality." What has never been seen before cannot be coded. By contrast, recent literary theory and criticism, which have pronounced the "death of the author," have raised to a very special plane of significance the role of the code.[2] Codes, whether of language, of body movement, of dress, or of food, are seen to be not only essential ingredients for communication, but also inescapable ones. They are essential for providing an interindividual, or intersubjective, basis for discourse. They are inescapable in that whatever is thought to be original, pure, or authentic is really only a "naturalized sign," one that denies its own arbitrariness and facticity for ideological purposes—witness the belief in modernism as a "natural" way of building, transcending the artificial conventions of "the styles"; or the conviction that the various signs of modernism, such as the picture window, the flat roof, or the unornamented use of "natural materials," came into being simply as the direct response to new conditions.

Duany and Plater-Zyberk have stressed the importance of the code for Seaside with an acute understanding of its poststructuralist implications (pp. 98–99). Its purpose in their view is social—"to make a public realm."[3] It defines the area of interindividuality. It prescribes the framework of the urban order at the same time as it defines certain types and elements of design and construction that fit into and articulate that order. It establishes a syntax, a grammar, and even suggests a vocabulary, in recognition of the fact that, to attain "a harmonious city," a commonly agreed upon language must be openly acknowledged. Perhaps most significantly, after drawing up the code, which is more a table than a written text, Duany and Plater-Zyberk declined to design any buildings themselves, as if to assure the "death of the author" in the "birth of the

4

reader," that is, those other architects and designers who would subsequently interpret the code.[4] The urban code of Seaside had, as Duany said, "very clear, physical prototypes in mind." One would have to go out of one's way to "misinterpret" the signs.[5]

There are actually two separate codes for Seaside, the urban code and the so-called architectural code. (I will refer to the differences later.) The urban code, which is the more general of the two, is considered by Duany and Plater-Zyberk to be the instrumental one, the one "necessary for the town to exist socially." The key factor in it is the social space of the street, what Louis Kahn called "the place of human agreement." "Our code is based on the making of public space; the datum is the streetline," Duany said. "Everything is fixed on the street."[6] In fact it was the decision to retain the county road, which runs along the beach, as the main thoroughfare of the town that allowed the plan finally to gel (pp. 91, 93). From it, a grid overlaid by diagonal avenues extends back inland and the hierarchy of street sizes differentially determines building setbacks, frontage widths, porch depths, as well as building heights.

A layout of streets can be read as the architectural equivalent of a code of social behavior. The street is like a sentence, the neighborhood a paragraph, the section a chapter, and the town a book. This is all the more important to insist upon since the street, or the lack thereof, is so easily "naturalized" as a sign. And we should not forget that the elimination of the street provided the ground for the institution of modern architecture. Still the most chilling description of the dissolution of this site of social discourse in favor of a

5

6

more atomized, privatized space is Le Corbusier's almost paranoid denunciation in "The Street" of 1929:

The street is no more than a trench, a deep cleft, a narrow passage. And although we have been accustomed to it for more than a thousand years, our hearts are always oppressed by the constriction of its enclosing walls.

The street is full of people: one must take care where one goes . . . .
. . . men and women are elbowing their way among them, . . .
and every aspect of human life pullulates throughout their length.
Those who have eyes in their heads can find plenty to amuse them in this sea of lusts and faces. It is better than the theatre, better than what we read in novels.

Nothing of all this exalts us with the joy that architecture provokes. There is . . . only pitying compassion born of the shock of encountering the faces of our fellows. . . .

The street wears us out.
And when all is said and done we have to admit it disgusts us.[7]

While I will not dwell here on the profoundly gendered character of this description—in which the dark cleft of the street becomes a site of filth and promiscuity, an image of the aggressive, fearsome female—it should nevertheless be borne in mind when contemplating the virginal, edenic antidote Le Corbusier offered in its stead.[8] In place of the street, Le Corbusier proposed a series of independent, "widely-spaced crystal towers" set in an "expanse of parks with a tossing sea of ver-dure" (fig. 4).[9] Freed from the terrifyingly constrictive walls of the street, one would come into direct contact with unspoiled nature, unmediated by traditional signs of architectural representation. Such a "radiant city" would become modern architecture's naturalized home. The sign of this new-found freedom to communicate directly with nature, to make architecture transparent

to its natural surroundings and thus give the individual immediate access to it and control over it, was the redefinition of the window in terms of the wall. Known as a strip-window, ribbon-window, *fenêtre en longueur*, or window-wall, the sign eventually became part of the domestic vocabulary as the picture window. Yet no doubt as a result of its quite literal transparency, this fundamental sign of modernism has never received the kind of critical attention accorded the other four signs in the aesthetic code Le Corbusier called his "five points."

The birth of the picture window was a direct outcome of the "death of the street."[10] There was no reason whatsoever to open up a building to the view if all that was to be seen was the dreary house across the street. Le Corbusier further recommended that his glass-walled buildings be "not oriented in alignment with the motor-roads or foot-paths" so as to prevent anything from obstructing the visual field.[11] Isolated in space and rotating around its own axis, each tower would control its own environment, just as its inhabitants would master it through their view. If the angles of rotation were carefully enough planned, no one would see anyone else, just nature—or what Le Corbusier soon came to designate, even more abstractly, as "sun, space, and greenery" (fig. 5).

The Seaside code gives special prominence to the relation between the traditional window and the street, recognizing the critical role the window plays in organizing the transition from public to private space. As I already indicated, there are, in effect, two codes operative at Seaside, the urban code and the so-called architectural code. The architectural code specifically governs materials, finishes, contractor's responsibilities,

7

8

and the like, while the urban code more generally deals with the relation between individual buildings and the infrastructure. One would therefore normally assume that window dimensions fall under the architectural code, along with such things as door types, roofing materials, siding patterns, and chimney details—and they do. But the key restriction relative to windows, that "openings be square or in proportion vertical"—in other words, *not* horizontal—is also included in the urban code. The only other purely architectural element (and here I am leaving out porches) that is covered in both codes is the roof, which must be "a gable or hip with a slope of 8 in 12," or, if flat, habitable as a deck "and enclosed by a continuous balustrade."

Both the roof and the window are signally characterizing elements of design. They establish the building's presence on the street as a social being. They both traditionally carry strong anthropomorphic references. For Frank Lloyd Wright, the roof type defined the house's individual character.[12] Like the color of one's hair, or the way it is done, or the hat worn on top of the head, the shape of the roof is an immediate indicator of personality. Erwin Panofsky's celebrated discussion of iconography begins with the tipping of a hat.[13] The windows of a building have most often been seen as its eyes and thus, by extension, the image of its soul. Windows are consequently more complex in their signification than roofs, for they are not only seen from (and through) the outside, but are also meant to be looked through from within.

When looked through from within, the shape of a window becomes particularly telling, for in relation to the viewer's entire body the window loses its transparency to the eye. A square window is probably the most analogous with the eye itself. Two square windows, one on either side of a door, make a face, or, as in Wright's Winslow House, a mask (fig. 6). A vertically proportioned window establishes a homologous relationship with the body standing in front of it. It is not by chance that the French call our American sash window a "guillotine window." The French window typically begins at the floor, like a door, and thus can be said to stand as the paradigmatic case—an opening through which the eye sees as the body moves with it. (When Marcel Duchamp blacked out the panes of a French window by pasting pieces of leather on the outside, he called the sculpture *Fresh Widow* [fig. 7].) The sash window functions like a synecdoche, condensing the role of the body in vision into its upper half, the symbolic seat of human understanding and intelligence.

The horizontal window, by contrast, suspends the relation to the body and offers up to the eye alone a distanced, more abstract field of vision (fig. 8). Its analogue is with the landscape itself, a relationship reinforced over the course of many centuries by the conventional use in Western art of the horizontal format for landscape painting (the vertical being reserved for portraits). Where the vertical window inscribes the body in the act of vision, and thereby establishes a coherent relation between inside and outside, the horizontal window alienates the one from the other by means of a transparency (as in diapositive) that reduces the world outside to a view.[14] The absoluteness of such a transparency is further secured by the elimination of mullions, which in the more traditional vertical or square window always asserted the physicality of the opening's surface.

9.
Louis Villela, display window,
B. Altman and Company, New York.
Interiors *(May 1945).*
10.
"Is there a Picture in your Picture
Window?" House Beautiful
(January 1950).

9

10

When one considers the relation between inside and outside, as established by the window, from a point of view outside the building, then the differences in shape of the opening take on even more explicit social and psychological definition. The issue, of course, has to do with privacy, exposure, and, in the extreme, voyeurism. Windows obviously let the view in. One might assume that the question is simply one of size, but that is clearly not the case. Vertical and square windows can only be so wide. They are limited, in effect, by their height, which is in turn limited by the floor-to-ceiling height, which has tended, in modern construction, to decrease or at least remain stable. Horizontal windows, on the other hand, are almost entirely free to expand in width as much as the architect deems fit, to the point where what had traditionally been private (the interior) is opened up to public scrutiny, unless some remedial measure is taken, all of which ultimately foregrounds issues of class, power, and gender.

One can easily trace the development of the large-scale picture window, or window-wall, of the modern house, beginning with the earliest examples soon after the turn of the century, to the availability of plate glass for domestic use. In the process of adaptation from commercial to domestic purposes, however, a primary reason for the commercial exploitation of plate glass was ignored or, at the very least, sublimated. One of the first important uses for plate glass, by the end of the nineteenth century, was to create the large display window, or show window, of the modern department store. These windows were designed to exhibit the goods that could be purchased inside in such a way as to seduce the generally female "window shopper" to enter the store (fig. 9). Mannequins were "dressed" in

11

12

settings resembling domestic situations, while objects might be grouped to form "still-lifes." An inordinately desirable interior world thus offered itself up to the possessive gaze of the onlooker through the exercise of certain means of control and manipulation responsive to the needs of the capitalist economy.

When the display window was transferred to the actual domestic environment, the social and psychological mechanisms of the market naturally had to be re-directed outward.[15] But what could never be adequately dealt with, except by such extraordinary means as wall-to-wall drapes or exterior baffles, was what later came to be called the "fish bowl" effect (fig. 10). Those who had been empowered with a sense of possession through their view became the objects of a view from the outside that effectively dispossessed them. Popular magazines like *House Beautiful* constantly warned that "a picture window should not be a 'show window.' . . . It should *not* turn a house into a gold fish bowl."[16]

Although the term "picture window," which dates from the late thirties, was specifically meant to define a horizontal pane of glass set in the wall, usually with openable vertical slots on either side (in effect, a domes-ticated "Chicago window"),[17] it appears to have been Mies who first made the literal connection between picture and window through the collaged photographic image. Many of his designs for country houses in Germany in the early thirties picture views of the landscape through large expanses of glass walls. These culminated in the project for the Stanley Resor House in Jackson Hole, Wyoming, of 1938, where photo-graphs of mountain scenes are substituted for the eleva-tions of the long walls, as if those pictures constituted

13

14

at the same time the physical fabric of the house and
the view seen from it (fig. 11). Architecture and nature
become totally transparent to one another. Structure is
rendered as a void, as merely cuts in the photograph.
No floor, no ceiling, no side walls are indicated. The
collaged elements float in the middle of the blank page,
eerily suspended in a disembodied abstract space,
addressing the sense of sight alone.

The Belgian Surrealist painter René Magritte probably
best captured the disorienting and alienating character
of the picture window in his numerous paintings of the
subject beginning in the 1930s (fig. 12). Typically, these
paintings, done in a *trompe l'oeil* style, show a window,
framed by curtains, within which is a picture on an
easel that supposedly depicts the part of the scene the
picture masks. Other versions, lacking the easel and
painting, simply show the glass of the window broken,
with the shards on the floor retaining the image they
would have revealed in the window. Despite the fact
that the typical window in Magritte's other renderings
of architectural scenes, like the windows in his own
house, were vertical French windows, all the ones in
this series of paintings are horizontal, with a segmental
lunette over them, obviously referring to the space of
the landscape and the sky above.

There are also a number of paintings by Magritte that
treat the themes of exposure, exhibitionism, and voyeurism, all in an architectural context. In the United
States, at about the same time, Edward Hopper made
the image of a naked or suggestively-clad woman in
front of an open window the sign of modern vulnerabil-
ity and of urban and small-town anomie (fig. 13). And
in what Mary Ann Doane has called the "paranoid
woman's films" of Hollywood of the 1940s, the window

Following pages
16.
Le Corbusier, sketch for his parents'
house, Vevey, Switzerland, 1923-25.
Le Corbusier, Une Petite Maison,
1923 *(1954).*
17.
Albrecht Dürer, Draftsman
Drawing a Nude, *Underweysung*
der Messung (1538).

18.
Le Corbusier, sketch plan for parents'
house, Vevey. Une Petite Maison,
1923 *(1954).*
19.
Le Corbusier: sketch of living room of
parents' house, Vevey. Une Petite
Maison, 1923 *(1954).*

15

"becomes a potential point of violence, intrusion and aggression" in its role as "the interface between inside and outside, the feminine space of the family and reproduction and the masculine space of production."[18] But it was Marcel Duchamp who most calculatedly deconstructed the mechanisms of display involved in the adoption of the "picture window" as the final term in the evolution of the Albertian paradigm of painting. *The Large Glass,* significantly subtitled *The Bride Stripped Bare by Her Bachelors, Even* (1915–22), focalizes the view on the surface of the glass itself, denying thereby any presumption of transparency, and defining the window as a place of arrested movement (fig. 14). The gendered structure of the mechanical transaction is inscribed in the superposed female and male forms, represented by the permeable shape of the Milky Way stretched out above the upright Malic Moulds. Duchamp's understanding of male voyeurism as a model for modern art ultimately resulted in the room housing the display of a spread-eagled, naked woman he constructed for his last work, the *Etant Donnés* (1946–66), which literally turns the spectator into a Peeping-Tom.

Few modern architects ever seem to have acknowledged the inherently paradoxical and illusory nature of transparency, as Magritte or Duchamp did. More to the point, few seem to have grasped the manipulative and alienating effect of the picture window. Indeed, most took it straight (fig. 15), so much so that the ideal of transparency, whether literal or phenomenal, became an unquestioned article of faith.[19] The authority of the view lay in the putative power of the contemplative subject. But the question rarely raised is, *Who* is

249

16

17

that subject and what does *it* represent?[20] To offer some preliminary answers to these questions, it seems worthwhile to spend a few moments in analyzing the small house Le Corbusier built for his parents, between 1923 and 1925, on Lake Geneva, and about which he later wrote a very telling description in the short book entitled *Une Petite Maison*.[21]

The search for a site with a view was the first step. A plan was readied in advance, much like loading a camera with film or, indeed, a gun with ammunition, so that when the site was sighted the plan could simply be discharged to the local contractor. Le Corbusier drew the moment of siting/sighting as a giant disembodied eye hovering beside a small, male figure (fig. 16). The eye/I directs its gaze toward the distant ridge of recumbent mountains seen on the horizon against the lower curve of the lake. The plot of ground, or *terrain*, is drawn along the lake shore as a thin rectangle with a slot through it. Upended and placed midway between the eye and the scene, the slotted frame acts as a kind of focal plane, reminding us of Renaissance images of perspectival construction, in which a gridded window pane was set up to record the intersection of the pyramid of vision culminating in the eye of the observer-artist (fig. 17).[22]

The analogy with one-point perspective is further developed in another small drawing on the following page of the book, which shows all the major highways of Europe converging on this single point of view. Then finally comes the plan of the house, partially enclosed by a protective wall, but with its single, thirty-five-foot-long picture window, across the lake front, directly facing the mountains on the far shore (fig. 18). *Its window*, as Le Corbusier called it, like *its eye*,

establishes absolute control over the view.[23] In turn, the plan of the house is drawn abstractly mirroring the view and submitting the serrated and curvaceous forms of the mountains to a controlling geometry, the Düreresque opposition of active and passive forces plainly describing an attitude toward the relation between art and nature that must surely be understood in gendered terms.

To announce the authority of the view, and thereby distinguish it from undifferentiated nature, Le Corbusier realized that it was necessary in part to frame it. To that effect, he punched a horizontal opening in the cloister-like wall of the garden at one "strategic point," as he put it, so as to make the view into a picture.[24] But that was only to be a kind of prologue. The main drama was reserved for the interior of the house. At the point where the cloister wall comes up to the edge of the house, the wall was drawn back, like the curtain of a stage, so that the view through the picture window from inside the house would be like that through a proscenium arch (fig. 19). Indeed, Le Corbusier described the action in theatrical terms: "Suddenly, the wall stops and the spectacle comes into view—light, space, the water, and the mountains . . . *Voilà*: the trick has been played!"[25]

Le Corbusier, however, would not admit that all was illusion, for he spoke of the window as literally "bringing the grandeur of a magnificent landscape into the house: the lake with its movements, the Alps with the miracle of their light."[26] The effect of transparency was such that, when you are inside the house, looking out, "the landscape 'is right there,' as if you were in the garden."[27] Carrying the analogy to its logical conclusion with an economy based on what Guy Debord

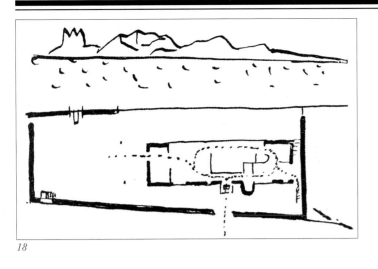

18

19

has more recently called the "commodity as spectacle,"[28] Le Corbusier declared that, with their new home, his parents had "*acquired* an incomparable and inalienable view." ("Sun, space, and greenery were *acquired*" in the bargain.)[29] In other words, with a little money down and a brilliant architect as an son, they secured permanent rights over a vast domain through the mere purchase of its view. And mastery of the view immediately conferred prestige and status on the house. In what is truly an extraordinary statement, Le Corbusier concluded that "the thirty-five-foot-long window" gave the house "*de la classe!*" (gave it "class!").[30] (Interestingly, the word "class" was translated in the accompanying English text of the book as "style.") Le Corbusier's explanation of his parents' "little house" perfectly summarizes the significance of the horizontal picture window for modern architecture. Let us simply note the various aspects in order. One: buildings are designed for individuals, and their private esthetic experience of the world is what must primarily be addressed by the architect. Two: that experience can fundamentally be reduced to the visual, or optical, sense. Three: the supply of a view confers the requisite return on an investment in a house. Four: the view provides a sense of control over a domain much larger than that literally paid for. Five: the disproportion between what is actually owned and what is felt to be within one's purview is understood in terms of the virtuality of the spectacle. Six: the substitution of a surrogate world, in the form of a commodity fetish, reminds one of the origin of the picture window in the commercial development of the department store display window. Seven: the abstraction of the view to the optical sense alone allows for the transparency that

is necessary to convince the viewer of the identity between nature and its artistic representation. Eight: the transcendent control of the view, reinforced by the privileged nature of its source, confers on any house graced with such a prospect an inherent sense of "class" (not to be confused with the superficial attributes of the "styles"). Nine: the sense of "class" is clearly linked to wealth in that only those who can afford the privacy of a view can avoid being spied on in return (or have an entire lake as well as a national boundary as a front yard). And ten: the exposure of the less fortunate and the less powerful to the gaze of others reveals a political dimension of vision that may most appropriately be characterized in terms of gender.

The proscription of the horizontal picture window in the Seaside urban code can be understood in the light of the concern of a postmodern generation with the social and psychological dimensions of perception, with the "ways of seeing," as John Berger has put it, rather than simply with what is seen.[31] As a result of the refusal to accept vision as merely a natural act, any sign of it, like the window, is "denaturalized," and such determining factors as money, gender, class, and power are foregrounded. To begin to understand how this might work in the case of Seaside, I think it would be extremely helpful to borrow some of the concepts and terminology relating to "vision" and "visuality" that have recently proved quite fruitful in the analysis of the pictorial arts, in particular, film, painting, and photography.
In his work on the origins of modern painting, Norman Bryson distinguishes between two paradigmatic ways of seeing as "the gaze" and "the glance,"

20

21

adapting for his purposes ideas from Sartre, Foucault, Berger, Mulvey, and especially the French psycho-analyst Jacques Lacan.[32] The gaze defines a transcendent, abstracting, immobile eye that views the world from a lofty Cartesian point of view. It is the eye posited by Renaissance perspective, an eye that controls, masters, and orders reality in a space of its own making that is outside time. "The logic of the Gaze," according to Bryson, "is subject to two great laws: the body (of the painter, of the viewer) is reduced to a single point . . . ; and the moment of the Gaze . . . is placed outside duration."[33] The glance, by contrast, is mobile, partial, and inferential, building up impressions over time. It is subject to the changing conditions around it. Fragmented and intermittent, it relies on a person's memories and other senses to form an image that is always shifting and can never be isolated or pinned down.

Where the gaze fastens on a *view*, the glance provides a *glimpse*. Where the gaze freezes reality into a spectacle to be appreciated at a distance, the glance incorporates aspects of the world seen close up into an ambient sense of environment.[34] The gaze positions its subject as spectator-owner so that the view becomes *his* possession. I purposely use the male possessive pronoun, for the aggressive position of the gaze as a historical construct of modern Western culture has generally been interpreted as implying the masculine point of view. "*Men act* and *women appear*," Berger noted. "Men look at women. Women watch themselves being looked at . . . . The surveyor of woman in herself is male: the surveyed female."[35] Although recent thinking has tended to question such an absolute identification of the gaze with the masculine subject, it

should be clear that, in its interactive relation of the body to the objects in the environment around it, the glance can still be said to represent its binary opposite in gendered terms.[36]

The most striking feature of Seaside, especially given its function as a vacation resort community, is its refusal to reduce the experience of living there to the acquisition of a view. This is in marked contrast not only to the nearby towns of Destin and Panama City (fig. 20), but to the typical postwar international resort, where bleacher-like slabs, or clusters of town houses, line up along the beachfront to face the view like sea gulls at an outgoing tide.[37] Normally, upon arriving at your destination, you get out of your car, go up to your unit with its large picture window facing the water, and capture the view in an instant (or Instamatic) (fig. 21). It is yours throughout the remainder of your stay, and you can even carry it back home with you as a photograph or a picture postcard. To buy into such a view, even on a time-sharing basis, is to "Own Your Piece of Heaven," as the promotional literature for the major new resort of Palmas del Mar, on the southeast coast of Puerto Rico, puts it.

At Seaside, a very different perceptual process takes place, one that is incremental and time-consuming. You do not immediately turn your back to the road and direct your attention out from the private space of your living room to the sea. The generous town square, surrounded by streets radiating from it, defines the larger communal environment in relation to the woods to the north. The streets are close enough to one another so that you tend to go places by foot (p. 73, fig. 14). You get a sense of the place bit by bit,

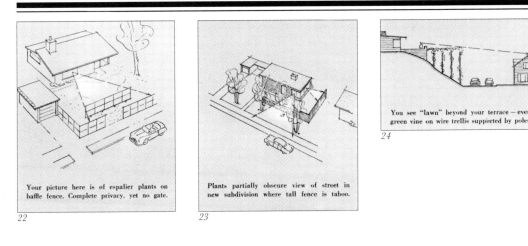

Your picture here is of espalier plants on baffle fence. Complete privacy, yet no gate.

22

Plants partially obscure view of street in new subdivision where tall fence is taboo.

23

You see "lawn" beyond your terrace — evergreen vine on wire trellis supported by poles.

24

Preceding page
20.
Condominium, Destin
(Photo: Neil Levine)
21.
"Choosing Your Accomodations,"
Pleasant Hawaiian Holiday,
Independent Hawaii (1989).

This page
22–24.
Suggestions for avoiding the "fish bowl" effect. House Beautiful (January 1950).

not just as one fast blur through a car window. The houses, fronted by porches and edged by picket fences, are extremely close to one another, which immediately puts you in mind of who your neighbors are and what your neighborhood is like. Inside your house, the intermittent window openings, some shaded by deep porches, allow glimpses of the street in front, or alleys to the side and rear. A scrub oak, some sand, a bit of sky, a latticework enclosure, or a neighbor's child shooting a water pistol appears like a moving figure in a scenario of summer vacation life that you slowly piece together from the interior world of your house. This is the world of the glance, of embodied vision. If you want an overall view of Seaside, you can get it from one of the myriad towers that the planners have encouraged homeowners to build. But it will always be a view *of* Seaside and not simply *from* Seaside. The towers function like those of medieval churches and cathedrals. The surrounding landscape is seen as an extension of the town, a frame around it. The town fills the foreground and acts as a *repoussoir* figure. The architecture does not disappear into the void, i.e., become part of nature, as in Mies's Resor House, but rather provides a center for a multifaceted visual experience of the landscape that is built up slowly over time. The very fact of having to climb the tower before being able to look around becomes a forceful reminder of the mobile, physically active character of vision understood in the glance.

The relation between interior and exterior space at Seaside, like that between town and surrounding landscape, is one of difference rather than sameness, of discontinuity rather than continuity; and it is this sense of

difference that is rediscovered as providing a communal meaning. The private world of the family inside the house is separated from the public world of the community outside, yet linked to it by means of the screened porch. This coded hierarchy of social behavior could only reoccur with the disappearance of the picture window. The anti-social character of large expanses of glass, which might not be terribly significant in houses for the very rich (viz., Mme. Savoie, Stanley Resor, or Philip Johnson), is particularly deleterious for communities housing those lower down the social and economic ladders. In order to preserve even a sense of vista within the typical subdivision, one would either have to give up any regular form of street pattern or else resort to some device or other to provide a kind of visual buffering, as these suggestions from *House Beautiful* in 1950 illustrate (fig. 22–24). The result has invariably been at the expense of the community, for whether the solution is to erect intermediate barriers or simply to turn the house's center of attention inward, the social space of the street is compromised and eroded until it literally becomes invisible (fig. 25).

Indeed, such a complete privatization of the public realm was the only way of dealing "architecturally" with the problem of exposure and voyeurism posed by the picture window. No doubt this is one of the reasons why the picture window, in particular, came to be seen in the postwar pop literature of the suburb as the very sign of the frustrated housewife. Home alone, almost all day, almost every day, waiting for her children to return from school and her husband from work, she could either "turn herself into an object," as Berger would say,[38] by standing in front of the living-room window, or deny herself that freedom and save her

25.

"Which twin has the privacy?"

House Beautiful *(January 1950).*

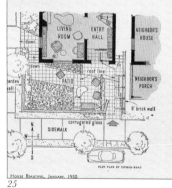

Which twin has the privacy?

by James Marston Fitch

Almost any city you can think of has whole neighborhoods of houses like these two. They're often structurally sound, well-located and cheap to buy. The big trouble is that they're crowded so close to each other and to the street that they offer you the privacy of a gold fish bowl. Yet see what a little imagination can do in selecting and remodeling such a house. The G. A. Gerbers bought this corner house in a Pennsylvania town. Then the architect performed some very skillful surgery. He stripped off the old front porch, threw a brick wall around the front corner of the lot, and brought in soil to raise the garden level up to that of the main floor.

You can see the result on the facing page. Instead of looking at cars, pedestrians, and other peoples' front porches, the Gerbers now look out on their own walled garden. And nobody looks in at them. This new garden gives them a pleasant outdoor sitting area for much of the year. It's tile paved for dry footing, partially roofed for shade and shower-protection. For an idea of what the garden has done to the *inside* of the house, see page 38.

HOUSE BEAUTIFUL, JANUARY, 1950

25

sense of self by retiring to the kitchen, which became the woman's social space. The title of John Keats's book *The Crack in the Picture Window* (1958) might therefore fittingly serve in any discussion of Seaside as an early warning sign of a postmodern social order in which relations of men and women, of power and authority, of money and class, are in process of negotiating new forms of balance.[39] In this regard, it may not be mere coincidence that no other project in contemporary architecture of comparable scale and significance to Seaside has so evenly distributed its overall planning and commissions for building to women and to men.

In its proscription of the picture window, the Seaside code helps restore a sense of balance by acknowledging and dealing with differences, both in human and architectural terms. In denaturalizing and thereby calling attention to one of the identifying signs of modernism, if not its fundamental one, the Seaside code allows us to see the degree to which certain structures of thought are implicit in particular modes of vision. The actual realization of the town following the rules of the code makes palpable the enormous differences between a *development* based on the gaze of modern architecture and a *community* resulting from the application of the principles of the glance. For this reason, the tower Leon Krier is to construct in the main square of Seaside will no doubt make a most evocative symbol for the town (pp. 168–171). It will bring together into a single community vantage point the various individual "views" that the modern picture window dispersed throughout space. And in dislocating the source of the view from the private to the public domain, it will reverse the roles figure and ground have generally assumed in modern architecture by foregrounding the streets and their containing walls of buildings and framing them in glimpses of the gulf and the woods.

As a final note, I should just like to add that Krier's tower also makes one wonder about the future of Seaside—what it will look like when looked down on in ten years or more. And this brings me back to the distinction its planners, Andres Duany and Elizabeth Plater-Zyberk, seem to be willing to make between the architectural and urban codes. Although what I have said here about the restriction on window shapes might lead one to believe that they are correct in claiming that the urban code is enough to ensure a continuity of their ideas over time, I would suggest that perhaps the vision they have of the community is too integral and too strong in their own minds to allow them to see how fragile it really is. The street must be a "place of human agreement" for it to continue to exist. But given the fact that the code specifically allows for the granting of all sorts of variances based on what is described as "architectural merit," but clearly can mean whatever is thought to be "interesting" or "exciting" in architectural design at the time, one can reasonably ask: When do individual initiative and experiment become factors in the erosion of the social fabric once again? When, in effect, does the authority of class, in the Corbusian sense, overtake the issue of style? Can attempts to be "modern"—especially when they are intentionally primitivizing or abstract (p. 78)—be contained within a code that was, in Duany's own words, written with "clear, physical prototypes in mind" in order to allow one to "go straight to the result"?

Perhaps so, if we take Deborah Berke's Modica Market or the Steven Holl building as borderline examples (p. 132–133, 172–177).[40] Still, one wonders how soon a bit of stretching of the code here or pushing of it there, in the name of neo-modernism, will result in the erosion of the very structure of the town the urban code is supposed to be able, in the abstract, to maintain. In a place with a climate like Seaside's, the picture window is not actually necessary, as Walter Chatham's house amply demonstrates, to cause the spilling over of the private into the public through a lack of definition between interior and exterior that is symptomatic of modern architecture's rejection of the street. It would indeed be an added bonus if Seaside were to prove, over the next decade, that modern architecture could come to terms with the street, and that the integration of "community and privacy" was not merely a rhetorical device of utopian modernism or just a nostalgic dream of the more recent past.[41] But the specter Duany raises of Seaside going high-rise "fifty years down the line" through the "power of money"[42] could in fact take place even sooner through the variances the code allows "on the basis of architectural merit." One should not forget that Le Corbusier's villas preceded his high rises by a quarter of a century, as did Mies's; and Wright built only one of his many high-rise projects (in Oklahoma), whereas Broadacre City is everywhere.

Notes

A number of people were extremely helpful in the preparation of this essay. Avery Gordon provided important research materials. She, Anna Chave, David Joselit, and Irene Winter made many valuable suggestions regarding the text. Andres Duany, Elizabeth Plater-Zyberk, Robert Davis, and David Mohney gave generously of their time and thought.

1.
John Morris Dixon, "Seaside Ascetic," *Progressive Architecture* 8 (August 1989): 59–67; and Beth Dunlop, "Coming of Age," *Architectural Record* 177 (July 1989): 96–103.

2.
See, e.g., Roland Barthes, "The Death of the Author," in *Image-Music-Text*, ed. and trans. Stephen Heath (1968; reprint, New York: Hill and Wang, 1977), 142–48; along with his *Elements of Semiology* (1964; reprint, Boston: Beacon Press, 1970).

3.
David Mohney, "Interview with Andres Duany," in *Seaside: Making a Town in America*, 63.

4.
The terms, of course, are Roland Barthes's (see Note 2 above).

5.
Mohney, "Interview with Andres Duany," 64. In this context, it is interesting to recall how Walter Chatham described his attitude toward the code in his attempt to produce an autonomous design for his own house: "I experimented to see how different a building I could design within the given stipulations. My house is meant to be a work of modern architecture" (quoted in an article by Carol Vogel, in the *New York Times Magazine* [30 April 1989, 56], aptly entitled "Double Standards").

6.
Mohney, "Interview with Andres Duany," 66.

7.
Le Corbusier, "The Street," in W. Boesiger and O. Stonorov, eds., *Le Corbusier et Pierre Jeanneret: Oeuvre Complète, vol. 1, 1910–1929* (1929; reprint, Zurich: Les Editions d'Architecture, 1964), 118.

8.
The gendered content of Le Corbusier's text was astutely pointed out to me by Anna Chave.

9.
Boesiger and Stonorov, *Oeuvre Complète, vol. 1, 1910–1929*, 118–19.

10.
This phrase was a chapter heading in Le Corbusier, *La Ville radieuse (The Radiant City)* (1933; reprint, New York: Orion Press, 1967), 119. Le Corbusier described the horizontal window as the essential factor in "instituting a new architecture" (Le Corbusier, *Une Maison-Un Palais: A la recherche d'une unité architecturale* [Paris: G. Crès, 1928], 106). It was, in his teleological view, simply "the inevitable consequence of reinforced concrete [construction]" (Le Corbusier, *Almanach d'architecture moderne* [Paris: G. Crès, 1925], 96).

11.
Boesiger and Stonorov, *Oeuvre Complète, vol. 1, 1910–1929*, 119.

12.
Frank Lloyd Wright, "In the Cause of Architecture," *Architectural Record* 23 (March 1908): 159.

13.
Erwin Panofsky, "Iconography and Iconology: An Introduction to the Study of Renaissance Art," in *Meaning and the Visual Arts* (1939; reprint, Garden City, NY: Doubleday Anchor, 1957), 26–28.

14.
For a related though somewhat different interpretation of this issue, see Bruno Reichlin, "The Pros and Cons of the Horizontal Window: The Perret-Le Corbusier Controversy,"

Daidalos: Berlin Architectural Journal 13 (15 September 1984): 65–78; as well as his more recent " 'Une petite maison' on Lake Leman: The Perret-Le Corbusier Controversy," *Lotus International* 60 (1989): esp. 63–71. Reichlin reinscribes Le Corbusier's critique of Perret in maintaining that the horizontal window not only lets in more light, but also denies the perspectival effect of a vertical opening which, in Perret's view, "reproduces an 'impression of complete space' because it permits a view of the street, the garden and the sky" (*Daidalos*, 72). This final conclusion, however, which wants to maintain the affinity of the horizontal window with twentieth-century notions of pictorial space (while at the same time preserving a "naturalistic" sense of transparency!) does not take into account the position of the subject, or observer, in relation to the window opening. Clearly, the degree of vertical expanse from ground to sky is dependent not on the *shape* of the window as much as on one's *distance* from it. On the other hand, it is the *shape*, and only the shape, of the window that determines our reading of it on the body/landscape axis outlined here.

15.
As early as 1906, The English Arts and Crafts architect M. H. Baillie Scott, concerned about the increased size of plate glass windows in "the modern villa," noted how "from the outside we have been made aware of these gashes in the structure, which reveal the window arranged, like a shop is, for outside effect. There is the table with its vase, the lace curtains, and the rest . . ." (*Houses and Gardens* [London: George Newnes, 1906], 66).

16.
Anon., "Is there a Picture in your Picture Window?" *House Beautiful* 92 (January 1950): 35.

17.
Robert Davis, whose grandfather owned one of the largest department stores in Birmingham, Alabama, recalls how his grandfather referred to the shop windows in his store as "picture windows" and how he eventually installed one of them in the living room of his own house.

18.
Mary Ann Doane, "The 'Woman's Film': Possession and Address," in M. A. Doane, Patricia Mellencamp, and Linda Williams, eds., *Re-vision: Essays in Feminist Film Criticism* (Frederick, MD and Los Angeles, CA: University Publications of America and The American Film Institute, 1984), p. 72. See also her book, *The Desire to Desire: The Woman's Film of the 1940s* (Bloomington and Indianapolis: Indiana University Press, 1987). I should like to thank Norman Bryson for suggesting the relevance of Doane's work to my argument. On the various complexities of coding the (urban) workplace male and the (suburban) home female, see Susan Saegert, "Masculine Cities and Feminine Suburbs: Polarized Ideas, Contradictory Realities," *Signs: Journal of Women in Culture and Society* 5 (Spring 1980, supplement): S96–S111.

19.
The key text here, of course, is Colin Rowe and Robert Slutzky, "Transparency: Literal and Phenomenal," originally published in 1963 (*Perspecta* 8) and reprinted in C. Rowe, *The Mathematics of the Ideal Villa and Other Essays* (Cambridge, MA: MIT Press, 1976), 159–83. Le Corbusier's caption for the sketch in fig. 15, as it appears in the *Oeuvre Complète*, *vol. 4, 1938-46* reads: "A frame all around! The four receding lines of a perspective! The room is set up facing the view. The entire landscape enters the room" (81). Le Corbusier's belief in transparency, i.e., that the view through the glass of the *fenêtre en longueur* provides an unmediated image of the world outside, can be likened to his belief that the use of *pilotis* left the ground beneath the house in its "natural" state. Without any apparent irony intended, he used the analogy of the shop window to describe the appearance of a building on *pilotis*: "Le bâtiment se présente comme un objet de vitrine sur un support d'étalage, il se lit *entier*" (Le Corbusier, *Précisions sur un état présent de l'architecture et de l'urbanisme* [Paris: G. Crès, 1930], 50, 60).

20.
Recently, some attention has begun to be focused on the problem. An issue of *Daidalos* (vol. 13 [September 1984]), dealing with relations between interior and exterior space, contains interesting articles by Norbert Miller, Kyra Stromberg, and Bruno Reichlin, on the subject of windows. Reichlin's studies of the "Perret-Le Corbusier Controversy" (see Note 14) offer penetrating insights into the "paradoxical nature" of the picture window, but without, in my view, problematizing the issue of the subject. In another recent essay on Le Corbusier, Beatriz Colomina acknowledges the distinction that any window effects "between being in a landscape and seeing it" in order to suggest that the transparency of Le Corbusier's horizontal window "works to put this condition, this caesura, in evidence" ("*L'Esprit Nouveau*: Architecture and *Publicité*," in B. Colomina, ed., *Architectureproduction* [New York: Princeton Architectural Press, 1988], esp. 95–99). Her conclusion, that Le

Corbusier's space is like that of the camera, decentering the subject and devaluing the controlling "eye of the beholder," seems to contradict Le Corbusier's constant assertion of the centrality of human vision— "the eye being the 'master of ceremonies,'" as he put it— in the organization and perception of architectural space (Le Corbusier, *The Modulor* [Cambridge, MA: Harvard University Press, 1958], 72–76.
21.
Le Corbusier, *Une Petite Maison, 1923* (Zurich: Girsberger, 1954). It is interesting that both Reichlin articles cited above (Note 14) take this house and book as their point of departure for discussing Le Corbusier's thinking about the horizontal window.
22.
Svetlana Alpers has offered a trenchant analysis of the gendered character of the Italian Renaissance concept of the perspectively ordered picture as a window onto the world. In reference to the Dürer print illustrated here, she says: "Dürer's woodcut tellingly reveals [this active

confidence in human powers] in the relationship of the male artist to the female observed who offers her naked body to him to draw. The attitude toward women in this art—toward the central image of the female nude in particular—is part and parcel of a commanding attitude toward the possession of the world" ("Art History and Its Exclusions: The Example of Dutch Art," in Norma Broude and Mary D. Garrard, eds., *Feminism and Art History: Questioning the Litany* [New York: Harper & Row, Icon Editions, 1982], 187).
23.
Le Corbusier, *Petite Maison*, 9.
24.
Ibid., 28.
25.
Ibid., 31. As Reichlin has also noted, Le Corbusier similarly described the long picture window of the house in theatrical terms, once as the "principal actor of the house" (34–35) and again as "the sole actor of the facade" (40).
26.
Le Corbusier, *Précisions*, 130.
27.
Le Corbusier, *Almanach*, 94.

28.
Guy Debord, *Society of the Spectacle* (1967; reprint, Detroit: Black & Red, 1977), 34ff.
29.
Le Corbusier, *Petite Maison*, 13–14.
30.
Ibid., 34.
31.
John Berger, *Ways of Seeing* (London and Harmondsworth: British Broadcasting Corporation and Penguin, 1972).
32.
Norman Bryson, *Vision and Painting: The Logic of the Gaze* (New Haven and London: Yale University Press, 1983), esp. 87–131.
33.
Ibid., 96.
34.
Kent Bloomer and Charles Moore have proposed a similar distinction: "When we consciously stare at an object the body boundary hardens and there is a heightened sense of separation, whereas a casual viewing weakens the sense of separation and encourages instead a psychic fusion with the subject" (Kent C. Bloomer and Charles W.

Moore, *Body, Memory and Architecture* [New Haven and London: Yale University Press, 1977], 43).

35.

Berger, *Ways of Seeing*, 47.

36.

See, e.g., E. Ann Kaplan, *Women and Film: Both Sides of the Camera* (New York: Methuen, 1983); Teresa de Lauretis, *Alice Doesn't: Feminism, Semiotics, Cinema* (Bloomington: Indiana University Press, 1984); and M. A. Doane, *Desire to Desire.*

37.

One can trace the concept back to Frank Lloyd Wright's design for the San Marcos-in-the-Desert Hotel, for the South Phoenix Mountains, of 1928–29, and Le Corbusier's project for the seaside community at Oued-Ouchaïa, outside Algiers, of 1932–34.

38.

Berger, *Ways of Seeing*, 47. The power of a window with a view to turn its intended subject into an object was commented on already early in the nineteenth century by the English poet John Keats. Writing to his wife Fanny, he remarked: "I should like the window to open onto the Lake of Geneva—and there I'd sit and read all day like a picture of somebody reading" (quoted in Kyra Stromberg, "The Window in the Picture—The Picture in the Window," *Daidalos* 13:60).

39.

John Keats, *The Crack in the Picture Window* (Boston: Houghton Mifflin, 1958). What eventually filled the crack in the window by replacing its opening onto the world with a less revealing, more privatized mode of contact, was the television.

40.

Even here, it is interesting to note how one refers to Deborah Berke's Modica Market and *the* Steven Holl Building in such a way as to assert the authorial character of the latter. This is all the more ironic, especially from the point of view of modernist rhetoric, since Berke's building is strikingly original whereas Holl's is clearly derived from Aldo Rossi.

41.

In retrospect, it is fascinating to note how little is said of community and how much is prescribed for the achievement of privacy in Serge Chermayeff and Christopher Alexander, *Community and Privacy: Toward a New Architecture of Humanism* (Garden City, NY: Doubleday and Company, 1963).

42.

Mohney, "Interview with Andres Duany," 73.

Architectural Code
Town of Seaside

General Provisions

1. Plans for all buildings, alterations and additions shall be submitted to the Seaside Architectural Review Committee (SARC) for approval. Variances shall be based on the basis of architectural merit and not on hardship.

2. In addition to the provisions of the Seaside Urban Code and these regulations, all construction is subject to the provisions of the Southern Standard Building Code and the C.A.B.O. One & Two Family Dwelling Code and all applicable state or county building codes. All review and inspection procedures described in these regulations and the design approval process are intended to assure compliance only with aesthetic considerations. Seaside Community Development Corporation, its affiliates, and the SARC are not responsible for design or construction defects or failure of the building to meet appropriate building codes.

3. All contractors shall be approved by the Seaside Administration. The general contractor and all his subcontractors shall be licensed as required by the Walton County Building Department. The general contractor shall warrant all materials and workmanship to be good quality and remain so for a period of one year. All contractors shall carry insurance as follows: The general contractor shall furnish to the owner evidence of the above coverage and shall secure the same from all subcontractors: Workmen's compensation: as required by law. Public Liability: $100,000 for one person, $300,000 for each accident occurrence. Property Damage: $50,000 for any one accident.

4. Construction Debris
Contractor shall furnish trash containers and, at all times, shall keep the premises free from accumulation of trash and scrap caused by construction. Trash shall not be allowed outside a designated trash and scrap area and any that does intrude beyond shall be cleaned up immediately. At completion of the work, all remaining trash and scrap shall be disposed of legally. Tools, construction equipment, machinery, and surplus materials shall be removed from the site. The Seaside Administration shall charge the contractor for any clean-up of contractor's building area.

5. Construction Noise and Pets
Construction activities shall not take place before noon on Saturdays, Sundays, and Holidays. Holiday hours shall be announced by the Seaside Administration. Radios are not allowed on construction sites. Domestic animals on construction sites must be on a leash or under the control of the owner at all times. The contractor is responsible for any noise or damage caused by any animal brought onto the site and for cleaning up after the animal. Contractor shall remove any pet if requested by the Seaside Administration.

6. A Certificate of Occupancy issued at the completion of the house by the Walton County Building Department will be necessary for a house to be placed on the rental program.

General Construction Requirements

1. There shall be no more than two dwelling units per lot.

2. Landscape
Existing vegetation shall remain undisturbed during construction, except for an area 4 feet beyond the perimeter of the building. Existing foliage shall be protected by roping it off from construction activities. It shall be protected from paint-over spray and from trash. Sod is not permitted. New planting materials shall be indigenous species or from the approved plant material list. Two trees of a designated species and caliper shall be planted in front of each cottage.

3. Footings
Foundations shall be typically wood piles 8" x 8" or round tip, clear pressure treated or penta-treated, elevating finish floor to 2' minimum above the existing grade. Crawl space beneath the floor joists shall be a minimum of 1'6". Restrictive heights shall be measured from the center line of the road. Pilings and structure to be certified by a structural engineer or architect registered in the State of Florida. Garages where permitted, shall have a concrete floor on grade with natural or painted CMU walls to the level of the base trim on the associated house, with wood structure above which shall be detailed in a manner similar to the house.

4. Roof Structure
Pitch above the main structure shall be 8 in 12. Roof pitch above porches and ancillary structures shall be 3 in 12. Monopitches shall not be permitted unless abutting vertical walls. Roof shall be symmetrical about their peaks. Flat roofs shall be permitted only when accessible from an adjacent enclosed space. Roof rafters shall be 2" x 6" minimum with 1'6" minimum overhang. Purlins shall be 2" x 2" or 2" x 4". No soffits are permitted. Fascias, if any, shall not completely cover rafter tails.

5. Exterior Cladding
All wood exposed to weather shall be of cedar, redwood, cypress, pressure treated pine, pine only when properly finished to prevent moisture from rotting the wood. Siding pattern may be rough or smooth: *106* dropsiding, 6" lapsiding, 6" shingle, vertical board and batten. Trim Pattern: shall be smooth planed: 2 x 4 or 2 x 6 at corners and openings: with caulked butt joints. Lattice Skirting: Strips shall have spacing no larger than 1/2". Chimneys shall be masonry, brick, or sheet metal. No wood chases or enclosures are permitted.

6. Fences
White painted wood picket fences are required at the street front and path front property lines except at Types I, II, and III. Type VII lots require picket fences at the front building setback line and at all other street front or path front lines. Individual fence patterns shall not replicate another on the same street. A gateway and entrance from all streets and footpaths shall be provided. White paint shall be selected from one of the following manufacturers' stock numbers: Benjamin Moore 103 and 105; Sherwin-Williams 107–8070; Glidden 2100, 3600, 3669; Pittsburgh 7245, 6–650; Richards 100, 300; Devoe 1501, 51501.

7. Exterior Doors

Wood: recessed ladderback; french door (true divided lites); "store door". Metal: "store door". Sliding glass doors shall be permitted only for access to baths and shall be located behind privacy screens, and shall be finished with white E.S.P. paint. Screen doors shall be of wood and of approved pattern. Garage doors: wood section, panel-type, overhead by Crawford, Overhead, or equal, eight-foot maximum width. Door Hardware Pattern: Schlage Plymouth, Baldwin 5030, Kwikset Standard, U.S. Lock Plymouth, or similar; no key in knobs allowed. Bright brass (lacquered finish not recommended) brushed chrome, brushed aluminum, or oiled bronze finish.

8. Windows

Pattern: Casement, awnings, or double hung. Individual windows and porch openings, when rectangular shall be square or vertical proportion not less than 1:1.5. Material: Wood or wood with metal or plastic cladding. No snap-in muntins permitted. Awning type windows of horizontal proportions may be used at clerestories. Fan windows, circle windows, stained glass, fixed glass, or other windows must be submitted for approval to the Seaside Architectural Review Committee. Screens Material: Dark grey fiberglass, aluminum, or copper screens. Wood or ESP white aluminum frames. Shutters must be operable.

9. Exterior Stairs and Railings

Stair stringers shall be notched to receive tread. Railings shall have a top and bottom rail, and pickets shall die into the bottom rail.

10. Privacy Screens

Materials: canvas or wood lattice with strips spaced a maximum of 1/2" apart.

11. Fasteners

All bolts, nails, staples, hinges, etc. exposed to the weather shall be hot-dipped galvanized steel, stainless steel, or brass. Contractor shall provide complete hurricane tie-down system consisting of anchor bolts, strapping, and clips as required for the particular connections within the structure.

12. Roof Cladding

Materials: wood shake, metal shingle, corrugated metal sheet, V-crimp metal sheet, or standing seam metal sheet. Metal roofs may not be painted. Batten rib seam roofs are not permitted. Horizontal seams shall be aligned.

13. Exterior Finishes

All exterior colors shall be approved by the Seaside Architectural Review Committee. Trim around openings shall be of a contrasting color in high gloss. Paint system used must be minimum: 1 coat oil based primer, 1 coat acrylic latex paint with Mildew Additive. Caulking shall be required around all exterior openings and at other necessary places where wood is jointed and shall be 100% acrylic or paintable silicon. When repainting, the original color scheme shall be repeated or a new color scheme shall be submitted for approval.

14. Service Lines

All electrical, telephone, and television service drops

shall be underground. For the convenience of owners and the Seaside rental program, a clearly marked valve to drain the house during freezing weather should be located in an accessible location. All supply lines must be sloped to drain that valve.

15. Exterior Lights

Exterior light fixtures shall use light bulbs of 40 watts or less. Lights shall be placed so that they do not shine directly at neighbors. All exterior fixtures shall be approved by the Seaside Architectural Review Committee prior to installation. All entries from streets or footpaths shall have at least one Progress P5204–38 "mushroom light" placed at the intersection of the path to the street or footpath so that light is cast on both the street or footpath and the entry. This light shall be controlled by a photocell.

16. Air Conditioning

Air-conditioning compressors shall be screened or fenced so that they are not visible from the adjacent property and so that the sound transmission to neighboring properties is minimized.

17. Driveway surfaces shall be: grey brick pavers, crushed oyster shell 4" thick compacted, or white clay over dolomite base.

18. Advertisement signs

(i.e. For Sale, Contractor, Architect, Real Estate, etc.), other than those furnished by Seaside, will not be allowed on lots. Exception: a single sign, no larger than 3 ft. x 3 ft., identifying the general contractor, only, will be allowed on lots under construction.

19. All houses must display street numbers using 3-inch to 4-inch brass numbers in a block-letter style. Numbers shall be placed on entry door post or header so as to be visible from the street.

N.B. This code is the latest version of a document originally written in 1980 and revised as conditions have warranted over the last ten years.

Notes on the Contributors

Kurt Andersen is a contributing editor to *Time* magazine for architecture and design, and a founding editor of *Spy* magazine. He has written for numerous magazines, contributed to television specials, and published several books on differing aspects of contemporary American life. He grew up in Omaha, attended Harvard College, and presently lives in Brooklyn.

Keller Easterling is an architect and playwright living in New York. She has earned two degrees from Princeton University, and has taught architecture at Pratt Institute, Parsons School of Design, and the New Jersey Institute of Technology. She is presently completing a video disk and a manuscript concerned with American suburbs from 1934–1960.

Neil Levine is an architectural historian, professor, and former Chairman of the Department of Fine Arts at Harvard University. He has written extensively on various subjects of nineteenth- and twentieth-century architecture, most notably Henri Labrouste and the École des Beaux-Arts, and Louis Kahn. He has just finished writing a major book on Frank Lloyd Wright.

David Mohney grew up in Michigan, and attended Cranbrook School, Harvard College and the School of Architecture at Princeton University. He was a lecturer and Fellow of the Institute for Architecture and Urban Studies, taught architecture at the Harvard Graduate School of Design, and maintains an active architectural practice in New York with his partner Joan Chan.

Credits and Addresses

Advance Design
Planning Service
E. E. Mitchell, J. W. Hunter,
T. R. Conklin
Stuart, FL
Doyle Residence, 1984
110 Savannah Street

Anthony Ames
Anthony Ames Architect
P. O. Box 54144
Atlanta, GA 30308
Crews House, 1988
Project

Tony Atkin
Tony Atkin and Associates
125 South Ninth Street, Suite 900
Philadelphia, PA 19107
Pensacola Street Beach Pavilion, 1987–89
Project architect: Sam Olshin

Steve Badanes
c/o Jersey Devil
P. O. Box 145
Stockton, NJ 08559
Natchez Street Beach Pavilion, 1988
Project
Renderings: Karl Westerback

Charles Barrett
3110 Segovia Street, Apt. 4
Coral Gables, FL 33134
Pool House, 1988–89
Project

Roberto M. Behar
P. O. Box 41–5114
Miami Beach, FL 33141
Motel Rooms, 1989
Project
Temple, 1989
Project
Collaborators: Fauziah Ab-Rahim,
Rafael Escalon

Deborah Berke
Carey McWhorter
Berke and McWhorter Architects
270 Lafayette Street, #1001
New York, NY 10012
Deborah Berke
Market Buildings, 1982
Town center
Hodges House, 1983
104 Tupelo Street
Averett Tower, 1984
109 Tupelo Street
Gray House, 1984
207 Tupelo Street
Wright House, 1984
101 Savannah Street
Assistant: Carey McWhorter
Sward House, 1985
118 Savannah Street
Assistants: Carey McWhorter
and Alan Dynerman
Gray House II, 1986
113 East Ruskin Street
Assistant: Carey McWhorter
Childs House, 1986
205 Savannah Street
Assistants: Ray Kinoshita
and Ann Marshall
Brinkman House, 1987
203 Savannah Street
Assistant: Melanie Hennigan
Sward House II, 1987
109 East Ruskin Street
Assistants: Carey McWhorter and
Melanie Hennigan
Averett House, 1987
109 Tupelo Street
Assistant: Melanie Hennigan
Jones Compound, 1987
206 Savannah Street
Assistant: Jeff Haines
Gray House III, 1987
111 East Ruskin Street
Assistants: Carey McWhorter
and Melanie Hennigan

*Modica Market Building and
Interior*, 1987–88
Town center
Assistants: Carey McWhorter,
Adam Yarinsky, Melanie
Hennigan, Destin Architectural
Group
Modica Market Meeting Room, 1988
Town center
Assistant: Carey McWhorter,
Chuck Wermer, Jaffe Acoustics
Carey McWhorter
Hudson House, 1985
115 Savannah Street
Berke and McWhorter
Schmidt House, 1990
Corner of Pensacola and
Butler Streets

Victor Bowman
Victor S. Bowman, Architects
P. O. Box 4741
Seaside, FL 32459
Fritze House, 1988–89
106 Tupelo Street
Mustachio House, 1989
Project
Ruskin Square Town Houses, 1990
Project
Bed and Breakfast, 1990
Project

Mark Breaux
Route 2
Box 834
Santa Rosa Beach, FL 32459
Breaux House, 1986
116 Forest Street

Ernesto Buch
31 High Street
New Haven, CT 06510
Tupelo Street Beach Pavilion, 1982
Public Works Building, 1984
Tupelo Street and Forest Avenue

Victoria Casasco
Victoria Casasco, Architect
320D Sunset Avenue
Venice, FL 90291
Appell House, 1987–89
110 East Ruskin Street
Walton-DeFuniak Library, 1987
Project
Bud and Alley's Oyster Bar, 1988
Town center

Joan Chan
David Mohney
Chan and Mohney Architecture
160 Fifth Avenue, Suite 800
New York, NY 10010
Restaurant Pavilion, 1987–89
Town center
Assistants: Chris Calott, Nathan
Cherry, Henri de Hahn, James
Mandle

Walter Chatham
Walter Chatham, Architect
225 Lafayette Street
New York, NY 10012
Town Hall 1985–91
Project
Chatham House, 1987–88
116 East Ruskin Street
Meyer House, 1987–88
212 Tupelo Street
Forsythe House, 1990–91
Ruskin Square
Pugin House, 1990–91
Ruskin Square

Tom Christ
Christ and Associates,
Architects and Planners
215 Mountain Drive, #109
Destin, FL 32541
Savannah Street Beach Pavillion, 1985
Hudson House, 1985–86
101 East Ruskin Street

Tucker House, 1986
204 Tupelo Street
Project assistant: Jamie Christ
Bruno House, 1986
103 Savannah Street

Stuart Cohen
Stuart Cohen and Associates
644 South Clark Street
Chicago, IL 60605
Anders Nereim
Anders Nereim Architects
4546 North Leavitt Street
Chicago, IL 60625
East Ruskin Street Beach Pavilion, 1985
Seaside Condominiums, 1986–87
Project
Avery Bed and Breakfast, 1986–87
Project

David Coleman
9 Marble Avenue
Burlington, VT 05401
Pavilion, 1991
Project

Caroline Constant
42 Union Park
Boston, MA 02108
Cameron Roberts
11 Beacon Street
Boston, MA 02108
Fire Station, 1983
Project

Cooper Johnson Smith
Architects
240 Plant Avenue, B101
Tampa, FL 33606
Cooper House I, 1987
116 Tupelo Street
Landscape Follies, 1989
Raeburn House, 1989
107 Odessa Street

Cooper House II, 1989–90
113 Odessa Street

Robert Davis
204 Seaside Avenue
Seaside, FL 32459
Dogtrot House, 1987–88
111 Quincy Circle
Assistant: Scott Merrill
Davis House, 1986–88,
204 Seaside Avenue
Assistant: John Seaborn
Post Office, 1985–86
Town center
Assistant: Robert Lamar

Andres Duany
Elizabeth Plater-Zyberk
Andres Duany and
Elizabeth Plater-Zyberk,
Architects and Town Planners
1023 Southwest 25th Avenue
Miami, FL 33135
Seaside Town Plan, 1979–82
Project team:
Andres Duany, Elizabeth Plater-
Zyberk, Robert Davis, Ernesto
Buch, Teofilo Victoria, Derrick
Smith, Maria De La Guardia,
Victoria Casasco, Luis Trelles,
and Daniel Broggi
Consultants:
Leon Krier, special consultant;
Berrett, Daffin, and Carlin, civil
engineering; Daryl Rose Davis,
interiors and color; Douglas
Duany, landscape; Rolando
Llanes and Rafael Portuondo,
renderers
Extensions to Seaside, 1990
Project team:
Andres Duany, Elizabeth Plater-
Zyberk, Robert Davis, Juan
Caruncho

Douglas Duany
688 Fernwood Road
Key Biscayne, FL 33109
Landscape Designs, 1980–82

Roger Ferri
Roger Ferri, Architect
270 Lafayette Street, Suite 604
New York, NY 10012
Odessa Street Beach Pavilion, 1989–91
Assistant: Maurice Saragoussi,
project manager; Robert Silman
Associates, structural engineering;
Warnerworks, Michael J. Warner,
construction.

Alex Gorlin
Alex Gorlin, Architect
380 Lafayette Street
New York, NY 10003
Leake House, 1991
Project
Assistant architect: Kevin Dakan
Town Center Building, 1987
Project

Louis Hiett
P. O. Box 4627
Seaside, FL 32459
Ashley House, 1986
106 East Ruskin Street
Hiett House, 1987–88
201 Seaside Avenue
Scottie's House, 1988–89
105 Pensacola Street

Steven Holl
Steven Holl, Architect
435 Hudson Street, 4th floor
New York, NY 10014
Hybrid Building, 1984–88
Town center
Assistants: Stephen Cassell,
Lorcan O'Herlihy, Peter Lynch,

Richard Warner, Philip Teft, and
Laurie Beckerman

Peter Horn
Mainframe Inc.
P. O. Box 4774
Santa Rosa Beach, FL 32459
Horn/Hodges House, 1988–89
214 Tupelo Street

Suellen Hudson
2100 Banquo's Trail
Pensacola, FL 32503
Hudson Houses, 1986–89
102 East Ruskin Street
110 Odessa Street
115 Forest Street
109 Pensacola Street

Leon Krier
16 Belsize Park, Hampstead
London, England
Krier/Wolff House, 1983–88
115 Tupelo Street
Tower, 1983–85
Project
Town Hall, 1986
Project
Church, 1988
Project

Robert Lamar
Lamar Design Associates
4227 North Davis, Building B
Pensacola, FL 32503
University Inn, 1984–85
Project
Winslett House, 1986
119 Savannah Street

Benoit Laurent
P. O. Box 4623
Santa Rosa Beach, FL 32459
Laurent House I, 1986

111 Savannah Street
Cone House, 1989
112 Odessa Street
Laurent House II, 1989–90
128 Forest Street

Joanna Lombard
3621 Bayview Road
Coconut Grove, FL 33133
Beach Club and Guest Cottages, 1982–83
Project

Rodolfo Machado
Jorge Silvetti
Machado and Silvetti Associates
560 Harrison Avenue
Boston, MA 02118
Downtown Building, 1990
Project

John Montague Massengale
Rural Route 2
95 Long Ridge Road
Bedford, NY 10506
Dawson House, 1987
54 Route 30–A
Atheneum Hotel, 1986–87
Project

Michael McDonough
Michael McDonough, Architect
131 Spring Street
New York, NY 10012
Jefferson House, 1985–86
Project
Honeymoon Cottage, 1985–86
Project
West Ruskin Street Beach Pavilion, 1986
Project

Scott Merrill
Scott Merrill, Architect
9300 North A1A, #201
Vero Beach, FL 32963
Hultquist House, 1989

122 Forest Street
Honeymoon Cottages, 1989
Route 30–A and East Ruskin Street
Ruskin Square, 1989
Project
Hinton House, 1989
104 West Ruskin Street
Doyle Cottage, 1989
209 Savannah Street
Williams House, 1989–90
52 Tupelo Street
Johnson House, 1989–90
Project
Motor Court and Mini-Storage, 1989–90
Quincy Circle
Corker House, 1990
54 Tupelo Street

Bill Murray
50 Bethkey Road
Killingworth, CT 06417
Murray House, 1986
107 Forest Street

Robert Orr
Robert Orr Architects
441 Chapel Street
New Haven, CT 06511
Melanie Taylor
Melanie Taylor and Associates
441 Chapel Street
New Haven, CT 06511
Rosewalk, 1984–86
Rosewalk Planned Neighborhood,
off Grove Alley

Rafael Pelli
68 Clark Street
New Haven, CT 06510
Dowler/Settle House, 1986–87
117 East Ruskin Street

Patrick Pinnell
School of Architecture
Yale University

180 York Street
New Haven, CT 06520
Heather Cass
Cass and Associates, Architects
1532 16th Street, NW
Washington, D.C. 20036
Church, 1985
Project

Derrick Smith
321 East 92nd Street, #2B
New York, NY 10128
Beach Pavilion, 1984–85
Project
Stein House, 1984
213 Tupelo Street
Miller House, 1985
102 Savannah Street
University Inn, 1985
Project
Pool Pavilion, 1986
Seaside Avenue

Robert A. M. Stern
Robert A. M. Stern, Architects
211 West 61st Street
New York, NY 10023
Seaside Hotel, 1984
Project
Architects-in-charge: John Ike,
Paul Whalen

Luis Trelles
Luis Trelles, Architect
2314 Ponce de Leon Boulevard
Suite 201
Coral Gables, FL 33134
Town House, 1990
Project

Teofilo Victoria
1025 Castile Avenue
Coral Gables, FL 33134
Market Pavilion, 1983
Town center

Brad and Heidi Wilkins
P. O. Box 4892
Santa Rosa Beach, FL 32459
Wilkins House, 1989
211 West Ruskin Street